Old Lerwick
People and Places

Douglas M. Sinclair

The Shetland Times Ltd.
Lerwick
2017

Old Lerwick - People and Places

First published 2017.

ISBN 978 1 910997 15 4

© Douglas M. Sinclair

Front Cover photograph © Shetland Museum and Archives

Douglas M. Sinclair is identified as the author of this work in accordance with the Copyright, Design and Patents Act 1988.

All rights reserved. No part of this publication may be reproduced, stored in a retrieval system, or transmitted, in any form, by any means, electronic, mechanical, photocopying, recording or otherwise, without the prior written permission of the publishers.

A CIP catalogue record for this book is available from the British Library.

Printed and published by
The Shetland Times Ltd,
Gremista, Lerwick, Shetland, ZE1 0PX.

Old Lerwick
People and Places

Contents

List of Illustrations	vii
Preface	xiii
Perspective View of Lerwick	xv
The Dutch Connection	1
The Coffee House	9
The Smallpox or 'Fever' Hospital	11
Twageos and Twageos House	15
Gressy Loan and Surrounding Area	19
Relics of Wartime	23
The Hostels – A Brief History	25
House of Charity	29
Missions to Seamen Institute (The Flying Angel)	33
Arthur Anderson and Cruising	37
The Knowe	41
The Old Manse	45
Stout's Court	51
Kveldsro	55
Craigie's Court and Quendale House	61
The Lodberrie	65
Bain's Court, Raven's Court, Water Lane and Irvinesgord	69
'Stebbagrind's House' or Seafield Court	73
The Queens Hotel	75
59 Commercial Street	81
61-63 Commercial Street	85
65 Commercial Street	87
Seaview Stores and Seaview House	89
The Old Tolbooth	93
Early Schools	99
The 1900 Storm	105
Da Auld Kirkyard	107
Da Big Kirk	113
St Clement's Church Hall	117
The Church of Scotland Canteen	119
Early Lerwick Inns and Hotels	121
Smugglers' Tunnels, or Cellars?	125
Christmas Shopping in the 1950s	135
Hame Wi Dee Lowrie	139
References	143
Index	161

Illustrations

	Perspective View of Lerwick	xv
1.	A Dutch Buis or Buss	1
2.	A Dutch race underway as illustrated by Davy Cooper	3
3.	The Dutchman's Leap at the Knab	3
4.	Bomschuit SCH68 Vrouw Kniertje. c.1908	4
5.	Hospital ship De Hoop in Lerwick Harbour. c.1904	4
6.	Two Dutchmen on Commercial Street at the Roost	5
7.	Steam luggers, sail luggers and bomshuits in Lerwick Harbour. c.1905	5
8.	A group of Dutch fishermen and boys with vessels in Lerwick Harbour	6
9.	Bomschuit SCH84	7
10.	Dutch fishermen on Commercial Street. 1920s	7
11.	Grootjes Poortje (Grandmother's Gate)	8
12.	The memorial in the lower part of the cemetery at the Knab	8
13.	Dutch fishermen sitting on the wall at the small boat harbour	9
14.	A group of Dutch fishermen outside the Albert Hall	10
15.	The Smallpox, or Fever Hospital, at the Knab. c.1902	11
16.	Johnnie Notions Camping Böd	12
17.	The hospital in a derelict state with the wooden hut built at the back in 1904 to receive smallpox patients. c.1910	14
18.	Twageos from the sea. Late 1880s	15
19.	Twageos House with Janet Courtney Hostel in the background. 1950s	16
20.	Papa Stour Sword Dancers at one of Miss Christina Jamieson's Shetland Folk Lore Society evenings in the grounds of Twageos House. c.1930	17
21.	Gressy Loan at the junction with Twageos Road. 1950s	17
22.	Twageos House under demolition and work commencing on the Coastguard Houses. February 1961	18
23.	The Knab and Cemetery, Gressy Loan and South Ness House. Late 1962	19
24.	Twageos Camp with South Ness House.	20
25.	Celebrating Victory in Europe with the effigy of Goering on top of the bonfire. May 1945	21
26.	Lieut. John Reade of the Pioneer Corps and his wife Joan outside South Ness House. 1945	22
27.	Aerial photograph of the Twageos area. 1962	23
28.	The Midgarth Maternity Annexe	24
29.	The Bruce Hostel	25
30.	The Janet Courtney Hostel	27
31.	The House of Charity, Knab Road. 1960	29
32.	St. Magnus Scottish Episcopal Church. c.1904	30
33.	Memorial to Lt. James W. Pochin, beside the Girlsta Loch. 2013	31
34.	The twin windows in memory of Lt. James W. Pochin, now in St Magnus Church. 2013	32
35.	The signature of the Strawberry incorporated into the Pochin window. 2013	32
36.	The Missions to Seamen 'Flying Angel' sign	33

37. The interior of St Michael's Mission Hall which opened in 1902 at Grantfield..34
38. In 1938 the Seamen's Church of St Peter was created in the Charlotte Street Mission Hall (now Havly) 35
39. The Norwegian Welfare Centre, Charlotte Street. 1960s................................35
40. Sjømannstua Havly in Mounthooly Street. Late 1980s...................................36
41. Reidar and Astrid Vetvik..36
42. Arthur Anderson from a portrait painted in 1850...37
43. The Böd of Gremista in 1953...37
44. Anderson Educational Institute. c.1904..38
45. The Widow's Homes, now Anderson Homes, as viewed from the shore. c.1904..39
46. P&O liner Viceroy of India in Lerwick Harbour. 1931..................................40
47. The Knowe with the Duke's Neb rock formation. 1989 41
48. Fred Irvine FRSA, c.1955 42
49. Muriel & Dennis Coutts. 2017...43
50. 'The Simmer Dim' from a painting by Fred Irvine 44
51. An illustration by Fred Irvine in the author's autograph book 44
52. The Old Manse in 2007..45
53. Looking towards the Old Manse from The Knowe. 1880s 46
54. Lower Leog. 1950s..47
55. Capt. William and Mrs Marion Sinclair with family dog Vera in the Old Manse. Mid 1960s..47
56. The Old Manse before the double windows on the front were added. c.1966..49
57. Looking south towards 17 Commercial Street, Da Roost Hoose. 1950s...........51
58. South Commercial Street looking towards the north 52
59. Miss Margaret Jamieson outside her shop at 15 Commercial Street. c.1910....52
60. Showing the demise of Stout's Court. 1962 54
61. Mr Arthur James Hay. c.1870s 55
62. Kveldsro House from the air. c.1966...55
63. On the lawn at Kveldsro. c.1930..56
64. The back garden, vegetable plot and greenhouse at Kveldsro House. c.1904...56
65. The Robertson family in front of Kveldsro Cottage. c.1900 56
66. Gilbert Robertson in front of Kveldsro House 57
67. Miss Margaret Elizabeth Hay in the greenhouse at Kveldsro House. c.1900 ...57
68. Jim & Irene's Kveldsro House Hotel logo shown on serviette, beer mat and cocktail stick 58
69. Irene and Jim Williamson with staff in 1975...58
70. Jim and Irene Williamson behind the bar in Kveldsro House Hotel, celebrating 20 years in business. 1988..59
71. The South End from the air. c.1966 60
72. Quendale House with the Craigie Stane and The Lodberrie. c.1966...............61
73. Lerwick Telephone Exchange switchboard in Quendale House 63
74. George Barrie and Beth Peterson at work. c.1970..63
75. The Craigie Coat of Arms..64
76. The Craigie Stane. 1920s..64
77. The Lodberrie with the Craigie Stane in the foreground. 2006......................65

78. The former Steamers' Store Lodberry and The Lodberrie 66
79. The Lodberrie and derelict shop before restoration. 1950s 67
80. Tammy Moncrieff 68
81. Bain's Court, Raven's Court, Water Lane and Lochend House. 1932 69
82. A portrait of Gilbert Bain 70
83. The upper part of Raven's Court with the west gable of Irvinesgord on the right. c.1880s 70
84. Print from lithograph entitled 'Lerwick', with shipping in the foreground in the mid-1880s, by John Irvine, RSA 71
85. Miss Beatrice Hunter in her garden at Irvinesgord. c.1960 71
86. Flats at Water Lane. 2017 72
87. Lochend House, Seawinds, Seafield Court, Scottshall Court and the Queens Hotel. Late 1990s 74
88. Bain's Beach with the Queens Hotel to its right. 75
89. Hay's Steps adjacent to Hay's Lodberry. 1880s 76
90. George H. B. Hay who created the Queens Hotel 76
91. The Old Tolbooth, Mr Levack's saddle shop and part of the Queens Hotel. Late 1870s 77
92. The Queens Hotel on the right showing the original entrance. c.1885 77
93. The south part of the hotel before the additional rooms were added in 1910 .. 78
94. A glass porch replaced the original entrance. 1950s 79
95. Re-roofing the building following the fire on 14th September 1987. December 1987 80
96. Hygienic Snack Bar advertisement as shown at the North Star Cinema 81
97. Old Tolbooth, Queens Hotel with Hay & Company's shop opposite and the Half Nyepkin. Late 1870s 81
98. William Brown grocer, Hay's Corner, the Old Tolbooth and the Queens Hotel. c.1885 82
99. The Queens Hotel with the newly built premises opposite, at 59 Commercial Street, which replaced Hay & Company's shop and the Half Nyepkin in 1892-93 83
100. Looking towards the entrance to the Snack Bar. 84
101. The much admired white horse model in the window of Mr Levack's saddle at 61 Commercial Street. Late 1870s 85
102. Hay & Company's buildings at 59 and 61 Commercial Street occupied by John Tait & Co. Late 1890s 86
103. Smith & Co, butchers and Economy Corner. Late 1950s 86
104. Smith & Co, the dairy and Economy Corner. Early 1950s 87
105. Seaview Stores with Smith & Co opposite. 1950s 89
106. The author and his sister Dorothy with Bill Smith of Smith & Co. Seaview Stores and the entrance to Seaview House are in the background. c.1966 90
107. Seaview Stores and Seaview House in May 1968, shortly before demolition 91
108. The Queens Hotel, RNMDSF, Seaview House with Jamieson's Knitwear and the Seamen's Home. 1950s 91

109. To allow the newly constructed Church Road to be continued down to join the Esplanade three buildings were demolished - Seaview Stores, Seaview House and the Seamen's Home. September 1968 92
110. An early view of the south end prior to the formation of the South Esplanade. 93
111. The stocks were situated in the structure to the right of the entrance to the Tolbooth. Early 1880s 95
112. The stocks as depicted by the artist Fred Irvine 95
113. Dutch fishermen waiting for their mail on a Sunday morning. c.1905 96
114. The last mail leaving the Post Office on Sunday, 8th May, 1910 97
115. One of the original clock faces on display inside the Toll Clock Shopping Centre. 2017 97
116. RNLI Lerwick Lifeboat Station. 2017 98
117. Clairmont Place, the Congregation Church, the Parochial School and row of houses in Mounthooly Street. Late 1880s 99
118. Parks at the Sletts. The Schoolhouse and Lerwick Public School, or 'Calderhead's School', and Lerwick Infant School 101
119. St. Magnus Scottish Episcopal Church and Schoolhouse. c.1904 101
120. Lerwick Central Public School. c. 1905 102
121. Looking towards Lerwick Central Public School from the Town Hall. c.1905 103
122. The South Esplanade after the 1900 storm. 105
123. The Old Tolbooth, Seaview House, the Seamen's Home and Sinclair's Beach. 1900 106
124. The Sea Road from in front of what is now Taing House looking towards Lerwick. 1900 106
125. Da Auld Kirkyard with Queens Lane on the left 107
126. The top of Queens Lane and Church Lane before Church Road was constructed. c.1960 109
127. Demolishing the old houses in Church Lane 109
128. Clearing Da Auld Kirkyard with St Olaf's Hall in the background 110
129. Inside the Old Cemetery, Knab Road, stand the 19 gravestones which were removed from Da Auld Kirkyard 111
130. The flagstone marked with a cross outside Krinigill, opposite the Masonic Hall. 2017 111
131. The top of Queens Lane and Church Road. 2017 112
132. Church Road car park, the site of Da Auld Kirkyard. 2017 112
133. Lerwick Parish Church. Early 1900s 113
134. The Parish manse - Clumlie. c.1904 114
135. Clumlie, St Magnus Scottish Episcopal Church and Schoolhouse, Kveldsro Cottage, the Rectory, the rear of Kveldsro House, Greenrig House and Upper Leog 114
136. The interior of Lerwick Parish Church before the stained glass windows were added. Late 1890s 115
137. St Clement's Hall, the Dutch Mission Church, which was built in 1911. 117

138. St Clement's Hall, the Church of Scotland canteen and the Circus Camp. 1946...........119
139. The County Library. c.1950 120
140. The Queens Hotel after the extension was built in 1910 but before the breakwater was constructed in 1914-15...........121
141. An illustration indicating that the Grand Hotel was now open. August 1887. 123
142. The Royal Hotel. c.1900...........123
143. Byrne's Temperance Hotel. c.1886...........124
144. The old town of Lerwick was built by smugglers. An illustration by Fred Irvine...........125
145. The entrance to a tunnel or cave was situated in the garden at the rear of the derelict Stout's House. 1962...........126
146. Looking south along Commercial Street towards the Sea Door, 12 Commercial Street and Da Roost Hoose. 1950s 127
147. Looking north along Commercial Street towards Nice Court, the Meeting House and Ross Court. 1950s...........127
148. The entrance to Raven's Court. Early 1960s...........128
149. The entrance to the tunnel at Seafield Court. 2010 128
150. The location of Murray's Hol. c.1880...........129
151. Underground passage discovered in 1967 during the construction of Church Road...........129
152. Fred Irvine's illustration showing what is now the Royal Bank of Scotland and P. L. Angus, The Shetland Bookshop. 1952...........130
153. The steps at Angus' Closs near Harrison Square. 2011 131
154. Fred Irvine's illustration showing suggested tunnel in front of M&Co. 1952..132
155. The manager of the Co-op, Jim Ganson, in underground passage in front of the shop on 27th March, 1976 134
156. Mrs Elizabeth J. Yates' Christmas advertisement 135
157. The entrance to Mrs Elizabeth J. Yates' shop...........136
158. R. Goudie & Son 136
159. Alex. Manson, H. & J. Greenwald, and James S. Smith, butcher...........137
160. A. W. Herd, butcher and M. & R. Georgeson, baker and confectioner. Late 1950s...........138
161. Peter Leisk & Co. 138
162. The Dreel Hall, now the Garrison Theatre. 1904...........141
163. The North Road, Burgess Street, 'Frankie's ' (Frank Sandison's shop) and Pig Street. 1904...........141
164. Lipton's, 173 Commercial Street. 1938 142
165. Ley's Hairdresser, 133 Commercial Street. 1938...........142

Photograph acknowledgement

The author's collection: 1, 3, 5, 7, 9, 11, 12, 16, 17, 18, 20, 28, 29, 32, 33, 34, 35, 36, 37, 39, 40, 42, 44, 45, 48, 50, 51, 52, 53, 55, 61, 63, 64, 65, 66, 67, 68, 77, 78, 80, 82, 84, 85, 86, 87, 89, 90, 91, 92, 93, 95, 97, 98, 99, 100, 101, 108, 110, 111, 112, 113, 114, 115, 116, 118, 120, 121, 122, 123, 124, 128, 129, 130, 131, 132, 133, 134, 135, 136, 137, 138, 139, 140, 141, 142, 143, 144, 149, 150, 152, 153, 154, 156, 159, 160, 162, 163, 165

Shetland Museum and Archives: Front cover, 4, 6, 8, 10, 14, 15, 24, 43, 58, 75, 76, 81, 83, 102, 107, 117, 147, 157, 158, 164

Courtesy of Shetland Archives: 31, 38

Courtesy of Elizabeth Angus: 13, 19, 21, 46, 54, 57, 79, 94, 103, 119, 126, 145, 146, 148

Courtesy of Aerofilms and Aero Pictorial Limited: 23, 27, 60

Dennis Coutts, photographer: 22, 30, 47, 56, 62, 71, 72, 109, 125, 127, 151, 155

John Coutts, photographer: 49

Kieran Murray, photographer: 88

Courtesy of Anna Simpson: 104, 105, 106

Courtesy of Ray Leask: 73, 74

Courtesy of James Winchester: 25, 26

Davy Cooper, illustrator: 2

Courtesy of Alister Smith: 96

Courtesy of Christine Johnson: 41

Courtesy of Joe Gray: 59

Courtesy of Jasmine Tulloch: 69

Courtesy of Irene Williamson: 70

Courtesy of Betty Tulloch: 161

PREFACE

Over a period of ten years I wrote a series of articles for the *Shetland Life* magazine under the heading 'The Past in Pictures'. Following positive feedback from many readers, not only from all over Shetland but indeed further afield, a Shetland Times staff member suggested that these articles could be reprinted in book form.

It soon became apparent that, with over one hundred pieces having been written, only some could be chosen and I decided to concentrate mainly on those covering Lerwick's south end for this publication. Inevitably some minor repetition of information proved unavoidable. A few articles were short and simply described a photograph while others consisted of two or three topics, which deserved to be separated. Several new photographs have been added.

In addition, having extensively covered Commercial Street in 'Early Inns and Hotels' and 'Smugglers' Tunnels or Cellars?' it seemed appropriate to include some articles referring to shops.

This book does not provide a comprehensive history of Old Lerwick and the format is intended to allow the reader to dip in at leisure and read any subject they find of interest.

The production of this publication has proved to be a very enjoyable and worthwhile experience and has awakened many memories. I was born during the Second World War at the historic south end of Lerwick, at Nice Court (now 1 Hayfield Court) to be precise. When I was four years old the family moved along the street to the Old Manse, believed to be the oldest inhabited house in Lerwick, but I still continued to visit my grandmother and great-aunts at Nice Court. Great-Aunt Mimie had a passion for Old Lerwick and I was fascinated by her collection of memorabilia including old books, programmes, postcards and photographs, which I ultimately inherited. She passed on her knowledge and instilled in me a deep and everlasting interest and affection for the buildings, streets, closes, lodberries and, last but not least, the many 'characters' that lived in 'Old Lerwick'.

I came in contact with a number of interesting and talented individuals who also lived at the south end. These included the artist Fred Irvine, who had his studio and home in The Knowe; Albert Bowie, who had his photographic studio at 8 Commercial Street; 'Auld Lowrie' Smith from Twageos Road, who built Shetland boats in his lodberry near the Craigie Stane; Tammie Moncrieff in The Lodberrie, who was a font of knowledge about Old Lerwick and all things nautical and Miss Beatrice Hunter who lived in Irvinesgord, situated to the north of Quendale House. She was the grandniece of artist John Irvine RSA. To me Irvinesgord was a veritable treasure house and contained numerous paintings of Lerwick by him.

All these people were keen to share their knowledge, and awakened in me an interest in social history, photography and art.

I am grateful to other Lerwegians who are no longer with us for sharing their knowledge and memories with me. These include Dr Mortimer Manson, Magnus Shearer, Noelle Gordon, Betty Simpson, Peter Smith, Ada Robertson, Tom Henderson, Erling J. F. Clausen, Andrew Williamson and John S. Johnston to name but a few.

I would like to thank Margaret Stuart Robertson for the many interesting chats and important documents and notes she shared with me regarding Old Lerwick, also Frances Watt, John H. Manson, Dennis Coutts, Betty Tulloch, Olivia Dalziel, John Tulloch, George Johnson, Irene Williamson, Mary Eunson, Thelma Malcolmson, Joe Gray, Anna and Charlie Simpson, Erik Moncrieff and Jimmy Winchester for providing valuable information.

Grateful thanks is due to Brian Smith, Angus Johnson, Blair Bruce and Mark Smith at Shetland Archives for their tolerance and patience while assisting with my many requests on numerous visits. Also the staff of The Shetland Times Ltd for the skilled workmanship demonstrated in reproduction of the photographs and text, to Charlotte Black of The Shetland Times for her enthusiasm and Linda Sutherland for her assistance.

Most of all I would like to acknowledge the indispensable assistance and unending support given by my wife Margaret, as it is entirely due to her encouragement and persistence that this publication has come about.

Douglas M. Sinclair

PERSPECTIVE VIEW OF LERWICK
from the North End by William Aberdeen in 1766

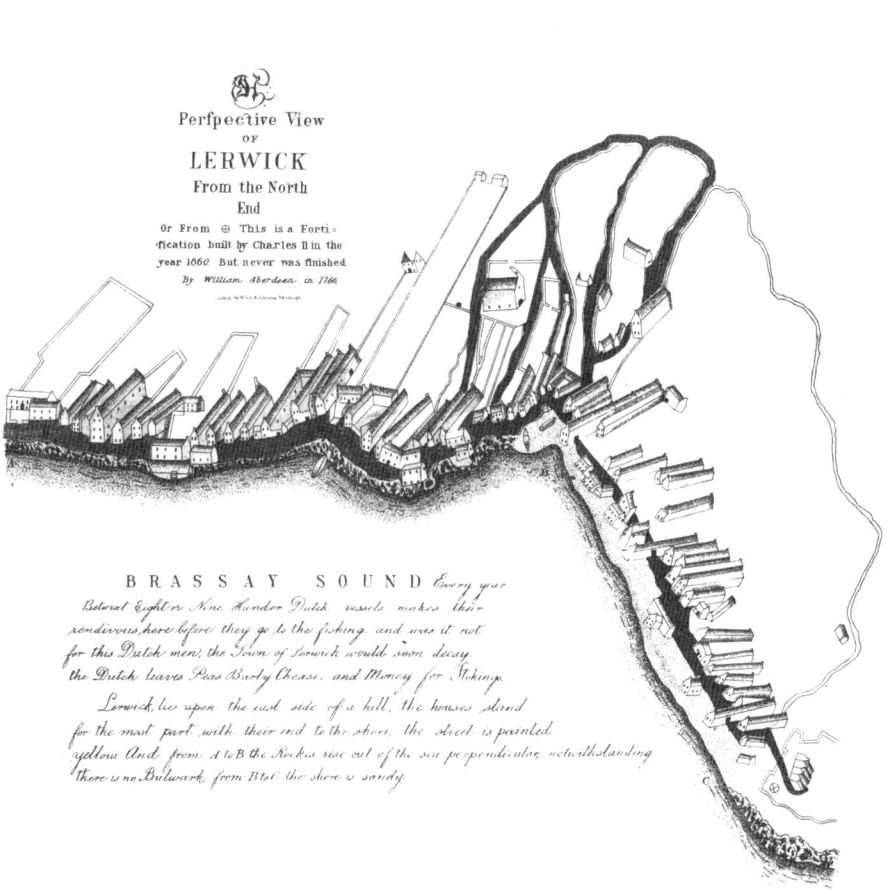

From Lerwick's beginnings in the 1640s, many substantial properties had been built by 1766 when William Aberdeen drew up this map. The street, or the Shore as it was called, was simply a path along the waterfront forming the lines of what was to become Commercial Street.

From what is now The Knowe along to where the Post Office stands was steep banks. Rocks along the shore can still be seen in the foundations of the sea walls at the Craigie Stane and Bain's Beach.

Another beach covered the area of the Market Cross, over which a burn flowed to the sea, and continued to the steep rocks below the Fort.

When looking at the map from the left, several buildings can be identified which have been mentioned in these articles such as Lower Leog, 7 Commercial Street, the Old Manse, and 10 Commercial Street which is on the lower side. Nice Court, Ross Court, Craigie's Court, Sand's Court, Raven's Court and Water Lane can all be seen, also a boat with steps leading to Lochend House opposite. The next building on the lower side is the first Tolbooth. Opposite on the corner is the Half Nyepkin – so named because of its shape resembling a napkin.

Da Auld Kirk, identified by its crooked steeple, is now part of the Masonic Hall. Boats are beached at the Market Cross and in an upwards direction from there are houses in what is now Law Lane. To the right of the boats is the present day Camera Centre.

There are three buildings with trances along the path or street until reaching the Fort. The first crossed at approximately where the Wine Shop is now situated, the second trance is believed to be at the south side of Pitt Lane and the third somewhere to the north of Hill Lane.

Examples of present day trances are between Smith of Lerwick and Halcrows Menswear at Norna's Court, and at the foot of Burns Lane adjacent to Mirrie Dancers Chocolatier.

The Dutch Connection

———•———

1. *A Dutch Buis or Buss*

It is a fact that Dutch fishermen were influential in the development of Lerwick. Around about 1469, fishermen from Holland first ventured to Shetland waters.[1]

By 1500 the Dutch buis, or buss, a slow-sailing two or three-masted vessel, generally 50 to 150 tons, was a familiar sight.[2] The buss could be called a type of factory ship. Herring was caught in the open sea by drift net, gutted on board then cured with salt in barrels before being transported back to Holland by the fast sailing vent-jagers.[3]

From as early as 1614, the Dutch were alleged to "frolic it on land", but the first substantial reference to market activity occurs in 1615. An edict issued from Scalloway, the capital at the time, stated that it was forbidden to trade at Bressay Sound and booths erected for the purpose were demolished. The first mention of Lerwick in a trade connection was in 1625 and, again due to the lawlessness associated with it in which drunkenness, theft, prostitution, assault and murder were all alleged, houses were once more razed to the ground. Despite this initial setback the town continued to grow and the first substantial merchants' houses appeared in the early 1640s.[4]

Trade was organised in what amounted to a fair at three localities – Bressay Sound, Hollanders' Knowe above Gulberwick, and Levenwick. Bressay Sound was the most popular.[5]

Britain fought three wars against the Dutch. A fort of sorts had just been built when, in 1653 during the first war, 94 English ships commanded by Admirals Deans and Monk anchored in Bressay Sound and troops were landed to garrison Scalloway Castle.

The building of a second fort was commenced in Lerwick during the Second Dutch War in 1665 against a possible invasion, with the garrison consisting of about 300 men under the command of Colonel William Sinclair of Ustaness, a Shetlander who had at his disposal some 20 to 30 guns. When peace was temporarily restored some three years later, building operation came to a halt and the soldiers departed.

The government chose not to place a garrison in Lerwick during the Third Dutch War, therefore in 1673, with the fort abandoned, Dutch sailors landed in Lerwick and burned the barracks and several houses.

This fort was completely repaired in 1781 and named Fort Charlotte after Queen Charlotte, the wife of King George III, the reigning monarch.[6]

The Rev. George Low wrote in 1774 that the whole time the Dutch fleet were in the harbour country people flocked to Lerwick with loads of coarse stockings, gloves, night caps, rugs and some articles of fresh provision to sell. Most could converse in Dutch, Danish and Norwegian and were paid in money.[7]

Bressay Sound – or 'Buishaven' – was an attractive rendezvous as it offered an excellent shelter for the crews while they waited for 24th June or Johnsmas, the Feast of St John, to commence fishing. In earlier times it was one of the stipulations in the Dutch fishing laws that herring ships must not shoot their nets before that date.[8] Although the law was abolished in the 1850s the tradition continued to be observed.

The fishermen and boys were at sea for long stretches at a time and the ships' surgeons recommended exercise when ashore. Locals took advantage of the situation and obtained much needed income from hiring Shetland ponies to the fishermen at "only a stiver a mile". (A Dutch stiver was 1/20th of a guilder at 5 cents.)

Pony races probably took place every summer but one such race, which took place in 1859, is graphically described. The Dutchmen who did not wish to join the races formed a ring in the wide part of Commercial Street and enjoyed themselves by dancing with one another to the music of an accordion. The race, described as primitive rather than orderly, started from near the old cemetery in Knab Road (Bullet Loan at that time), to the point of the Knab and back again.

Mounting the ponies was a great source of amusement as the riders frequently tried to climb on from the tail. They were assisted by young women, mainly from the Sound area, who looked after the ponies. When perhaps eight or ten were ready the race began with a corresponding number of girls running behind with whips to keep the speed up and to catch the riders who invariably fell off within a few minutes. The inexperienced riders either held on with both hands to the saddle, if they had one; wrapped their arms around the animal's neck, or held on to the mane in one hand and the tail in the other. They roared as the race progressed. Often a mischievous young local boy would jump out and startle a pony but, undaunted, the fallen rider would remount and set off again to catch up with the others.[9]

2. A Dutch race underway as illustrated by Davy Cooper

During one of these races (the year is not recorded) all went well until one terrified rider with equally terrified pony, out of control, could not stop in time and went over the cliff at the Knab at the place described as a precipice and deep chasm. Both rider and pony were dashed on the rocks below and neither survived. To this day it is still called the 'Dutchman's Leap'.[10]

After 1866 the busses were replaced by the herring-lugger, and cotton had replaced hemp nets. At the end of the century the fleet numbered 200 luggers, mainly from Vlaardingen. The fishing villages along the coast, in particular Scheveningen and Katwijk, shared in this prosperity. Fishermen from these villages used the bomschuit or bom, a type of flat-bottomed vessel, which had the advantage of being able to fish in shallow

3. The Dutchman's Leap at the Knab

4. *Bomschuit SCH68 Vrouw Kniertje. c.1908*

5. *Hospital ship De Hoop in Lerwick Harbour c. 1904*

water and could easily be beached, as some of these places had no harbour.[11]

Beaching also allowed repairs to be undertaken and a favourite location in Lerwick was Skippadock,[12] sometimes referred to as Skibbadock, nowadays the area of the West Dock. Jakob Jakobsen, the Faroese scholar, defines the word skib or skibb – "to cleanse by scraping, to a ship's bottom".[13]

Ties with Lerwick became even stronger than before. Unfortunately there were often accidents at sea. Hospital ships accompanied the fishing fleet, in particular *De Hoop* (*The Hope*), which was introduced in 1898. She was a regular visitor to Lerwick.[14] Fishermen who did not survive, whether by accident or illness, were frequently buried in the lower cemetery at the Knab, where a memorial was erected in 1978.[15]

Some years ago a Dutch visitor said that his father, grandfather and great-grandfather had all fished in Shetland waters and that to arrive in Bressay Sound carried a certain status. There was a belief that they were not real herring fishermen unless they had visited "De Baai van Lerwick".[16]

During the fishing season Commercial Street resounded to the click-clack of klompen – the wooden clogs worn by cigar smoking Dutch fishermen. It was said that they caused most of the congestion on Commercial Street as one Dutchman took up as much room as did two ordinary people.[17] They dressed in baggy trousers and carried brightly coloured handkerchiefs filled with their favourite peppermints they bought from local shops, one of which was George Inkster, grocer, tea dealer and confectioner.[18] His shop at 96 Commercial Street is now Loose Ends, formerly the Medical Hall. Another favourite purchase was Wally dog ornaments, which they termed 'Shetland spaniels'.[19] They also brought home bags of English flour and the bags were washed and made into frock coats and put into the tan-kettle. The boys who went to sea for the first or second time used to wear them on board.[20]

In 1897 a fleet of 608 ships (283 luggers and 325 boms), manned by between four and five thousand men, were herring fishing in the North Sea. On 20th June, on the Sunday before Johnsmas, between 130 and 150 Dutch vessels were in Lerwick. On board were nearly 1,000 men from Vlaardingen, Maasluis, Schiedam, Ter Heijde, Scheveningen, Katwijk, Noordwijk, Egmond, Zandvoort, Harderwijk, Rotterdam and Friesland, also a few from Germany. Over 900 people attended the evening service in Lerwick Parish Church to hear the Rev. L. van der Valk from the Reform Church in Scheveningen preach. Included were some local people who had joined the congregation to hear the singing, and many could understand the Dutch language.

The Rev. van der Valk reported the opening of Gilbertson Public Park and Queen Victoria's diamond jubilee celebrations during his four-week visit in 1897, and 500 Dutchmen joined locals at Fort Charlotte for the thanksgiving service.[21]

In 1898 Lerwick Parish Church, later named St Columba's, rented the Coffee

6. *Two Dutchmen on Commercial Street at the Roost. The building behind them was that of James Bain, Tailor. In 1905 this whole block was purchased by E. S. Reid Tait & Co and replaced by the building now occupied by Ninian and Aurora. The frontage of the building on the right was set back in 1936 and is now part of Conochies. c.1900*

7. *Steam luggers, sail luggers and bomshuits in Lerwick Harbour. c.1905*

8. *A group of Dutch fishermen and boys with vessels in Lerwick Harbour*

Hoose, previously the Albert Café, situated at the top of Garthspool Road on the east side at its junction with North Road.[22] It was renamed the Albert Hall and made available to the Dutch fishermen who used it extensively. Here they could read newspapers, write letters and rest. Coffee and cocoa were provided free of charge, while the Dutch flag flew over 'De Albert Hall' and a portrait of their queen hung inside on the wall. Short services took place on the days that fishermen were present. The Rev. van der Valk made at least four visits to Shetland and preached in the hall.[23]

Under the auspices of Lerwick Parish Church, St Clement's Hall was constructed in St Olaf Street and was opened on 17th May, 1911, by the Rev. A. J. Campbell for use by the Dutch as a Mission Church,[24] and therefore the Albert Hall was no longer needed. On 2nd July, 1911, Dom. S. Datema and G. H. van de Vegte, who were in Lerwick providing services to the Dutch fishermen, ordained the stained glass window in St Clement's Hall that had been presented by the Reformed Church in Holland to the building committee of the Parish Church.[25]

By 1919 the bomschuit had been almost entirely replaced by the sail lugger and steam lugger. An economic crisis resulted in an annual reduction of the Dutch herring fleet and by 1930 the sail lugger had almost disappeared. Distant fishing grounds were rejected as supply was adapted to demand and greater engine capacity enabled fishermen to spend weekends at home. The annual contact between Holland and Shetland decreased and became intermittent. The Second World War changed the situation even further, although small numbers of Dutch fishing vessels still continued to visit Lerwick up to the early 1960s. Nowadays there are a constant number of Dutch yachts arriving in the harbour during the summer months and the links with the Netherlands are maintained.[26]

In June 2007, the *Togo*, a former Dutch fishing boat converted for cruises, paid a visit during the Johnsmas Foy. One of the crew, a retired fisherman, mentioned that Dutch fishermen used to throw coins at a rock on leaving[27] Lerwick at the beginning of the season to 'buy' good luck at the fishing grounds, but was unsure where this rock was situated. He promised that on his return to Katwijk he would endeavour to obtain further information.

A copy of an article written in Dutch, along with an English translation, duly arrived containing a photo showing the arch below Bressay Lighthouse with the caption Grootjes Poortje or 'Grandmother's Gate'. The article explained that when a vessel reached approximately the position shown by the boat in the photograph, the opening in the rock was visible and revealed Grandmother's Gate. At this spot coins were discreetly thrown overboard and the deeply religious Protestant fisherman hoped that his fellow crewmen did not see the deed as the superstition was frowned upon.[28]

9. Bomschuit SCH84

10. *Dutch fishermen on Commercial Street, 1920s*

11. Grootjes Poortje (Grandmother's Gate)

Another Dutch visitor was Henk Grootveld, who came to Lerwick in June 2012 to list the fishermen from Scheveningen who had lost their lives in Shetland waters and were buried in the lower cemetery at the Knab. Twelve men were identified and Mr Grootveld, on behalf of the Dutch memorial committee of which he is chairman, held a short service at the Dutch memorial in the cemetery. Also attending was Mr Grootveld's wife Marianne, former SIC councillor Jim Henry, the author and his wife Margaret and multi-linguist Derick Herning. A wreath was laid then Henk and Derick sang the national hymn of the Netherlands.[29]

The names of the fishermen have been added to the wall erected along the waterfront at Scheveningen in memory of all their local fishermen who have died at sea since 1813.[30]

12. The memorial in the lower part of the cemetery at the Knab provided by a group of Dutch people and unveiled on 10th June, 1978, by Mr J. den Dulk

The Coffee House

●

13. *Dutch fishermen sitting on the wall at the small boat harbour*

In 1883 John Bruce Leask inherited the area known as Garthspool from his uncle, Joseph Leask of Sand. He subsequently bought properties in the area and built the tenement at Garthspool Place,[1] better known locally as Da Stane Hoose.

In 1884 an advertisement announced that the Garthspool Reading Room would open to the public on 29th November, to provide "*an evening resort for Fishermen and the Working Classes*" and a liberal supply of newspapers and games would be available. The admission charge was one penny, a contribution towards lighting and upkeep. Unfortunately there is no reference to its exact location, however the Coffee House is first mentioned in 1885 when a Mrs Ingram was tenant[2] and this may well have been the same establishment. It was situated at the top of Garthspool Road, on the east side, presently the site of Allied Taxis.

Although owned by John Leask the Coffee House was occupied by a number of Lerwick grocers until 1890. John Byrne, who owned the Albert Hotel situated near the Market Cross (at the rear of The Lounge Bar and accessible from Pirate Lane), then rented the building and renamed it the Albert Café. It was reported that temperance drinks would be supplied at all hours, also newspapers and periodicals.[3]

Between 1893 and 1894[4] the building was vacant until bought by Andrew Smith. It was renamed the Meeting House by James Pearson, who occupied the building until 1898.[5] Lerwick Parish Church then became the tenant and it was renamed the Albert Hall, but the former original name stuck and it continued to be called 'Da Coffee Hoose'.

In 1901 meetings were held in the hall during the summer and were largely attended by the fishing community. Sunday school was at 3.00pm, there was a weekly night service and also Band of Hope meetings.[6]

The church offered the Albert Hall as a sanctuary for Dutch fishermen and it became a very popular venue. Letters were written home, there were newspapers available, while a cup of coffee or cocoa was available free of charge. A portrait of the Dutch queen hung on the wall and the tricolour flew over the roof. A verse was read from the bible to the fishermen, followed by a few words and a prayer. The Dutch Reform Marine Churches in Scheveningen requested that the Rev. L. van der Valk be sent to Shetland to provide advice and assistance to the fishermen. It would appear, as already mentioned, that he visited the islands on at least four occasions.[7]

In 1911 St Clement's Church Hall in St Olaf Street, erected by Lerwick Parish Church, was opened for use by the Dutch fishermen and also as a church hall[8] and the Albert Hall was therefore no longer required by the church.

Subsequently the hall was used by the London City Mission and later by the Boy Scouts. In 1914 it became a private dwelling house but was still referred to as Da Coffee Hoose.[9]

14. *A group of Dutch fishermen outside the Albert Hall and in the centre of the group is the Rev. Van der Valk wearing a top hat. The row of houses next to the hall is Klondyke Cottages, occupied by Lerwick fishermen and their families.*

The Smallpox or 'Fever' Hospital

15. *The Smallpox, or Fever Hospital, at the Knab. c.1902*

The first hospitals in Lerwick are believed to have been used to treat sick and injured Dutch fishermen. It has been handed down that around 1690 a Royal Dutch Hospital was in the building now housing The Camera Shop on Commercial Street.[1]

A Zeikenhuis – "the house that has been used as a hospital" – is marked on an 18th-century Dutch map and appears to be situated to the west of the Sea Road, in the vicinity of West Hall.[2]

The next hospital did not come into existence until 1841.

Life in Shetland at the beginning of the 18th century was dominated by serious infectious diseases such as typhus and smallpox. The first mention of smallpox occurring in Shetland was when the Rev. John Brand wrote, in 1701, that a gentleman's son lately returning from south with the disease called along Fair Isle on his way north, resulting in the subsequent deaths of two thirds of the population there.[3]

Smallpox quickly spread throughout Shetland as the population had no immunity from it. On one Sunday, 90 people suffering from the disease were prayed for in the Lerwick Kirk (now part of the Masonic Hall), whereas a few weeks previously there had been none.[4]

There was another epidemic in 1720, which was so fatal that it was referred to as the 'mortal pocks'. In Foula, the mortality was so great that there were scarcely people left alive to bury the dead. There were further outbreaks in 1740 and 1760. In 1761, inoculation was introduced but was a hazardous operation, and due to the high fee charged it was confined to the higher ranks. As a consequence no more than a dozen people were treated.[5]

The population of Lerwick was estimated to be between 650 and 700 in 1762.[6] In 1769 there was yet another outbreak and the following year a resident surgeon inoculated several hundred people. Inoculation was thereafter successfully practised, even by non-medical people, the most notable being an Eshaness man, John Williamson, otherwise known as Johnnie Notions, who will be remembered for his pioneering work. Several thousands were inoculated by him and all survived.[7] He invented an improved method of inoculation and had it not been superseded by vaccination would have proved one of the most valuable discoveries in modern medicine.[8]

Edward Jenner, an English physician and scientist, developed smallpox vaccine in 1796. He knew that country people believed that those who caught cowpox would never catch smallpox. They were proved correct when he vaccinated a boy with cowpox taken from a milkmaid and the boy was then immune to smallpox.[9]

An article by local surgeon Gilbert W. Spence M.D. stated that vaccination came to Shetland in 1804.[10]

The early 19th century saw a dramatic increase in the population of Lerwick and many of the houses, particularly in the lanes, became seriously overcrowded. For example, in 1833 there were 250 people living in South Kirk Closs (now part of Church Road), giving an average of 16 people per house. In one house there were 38 residents.[11]

Concern was raised with regard to the sanitary arrangements that existed, which was a breeding ground for serious infectious diseases. A letter to the 'Shetland Advertiser' on the 1st September, 1862, by Gilbert W. Spence M.D., described the reaction of local people over 20 years earlier: "*Previous to the year 1839, I well remember what took place*

16. *Johnnie Notions Camping Böd. It is believed that John Williamson, or Johnnie Notions, was born in this house at Hamnavoe, Eshaness in 1740*

whenever smallpox or fever broke out in any part of Lerwick. There was a panic, the neighbours fled if they could find a refuge, which was seldom obtainable, for they were shunned and dreaded as plague stricken."

He went on to say that the people from the country were even more afraid, and always asked before venturing down any lane: "*Is dis a fivvery closs?*"

They carried a small bit of camphor in a small bag around their necks. They dreaded being 'smit' but in spite of the camphor they frequently caught whatever was going about and died.

The need for a hospital was apparent to provide treatment and to isolate and prevent epidemics of infectious diseases. The Heritors provided a former croft house and outhouse located at the South Ness Park, near the Knab,[12] for use as a temporary hospital and, in June 1841, two children suffering from smallpox were admitted. This building was situated in the upper part of the present cemetery and was rented from the owner, Mr William Merrylees, at a yearly cost of £1 10shillings (£1.50).[13]

In 1845 a storeroom and kitchen was added, funded by public subscription, and it became a permanent four-bedded 'fever' hospital,[14] primarily used for victims of smallpox, many of whom were seamen and fishermen admitted from the large variety of ships visiting Lerwick. A nurse was employed to look after any patients as well as keeping the hospital well aired and clean. An incident of theft that occurred in 1851 reveals that Barbara Brock was a nurse there.[15]

Dr John Cowie reported that by 1849 the state of sanitation in Lerwick had not improved. There were open spaces of ground containing large quantities of stagnant water mixed with animal and vegetable substances in a rotting state, also heaps of manure within a few feet of the doors of the dwelling houses. An open main running between Hill Lane and Burns Lane filled with fish offal and other putrid matter gave off a vile stench.[16]

By 1870 the cemetery in Knab Road, which was created in 1834[17], was rapidly filling. On 27th November, 1872, the trustees for the Feuars and Heritors of Lerwick sold ground in the South Ness Park to the Parochial Board as a site for a new cemetery. The hospital and ground surrounding it were included in the sale, but only for the purpose of being used for hospital accommodation and sufficient access to the new burial ground being reserved.[18]

The following year a seaman who had come from Greenock, where smallpox had been present, was admitted with the disease and very soon after he died. Within two hours of his death he was buried. At the time it was reported that due to the construction of the doors it was impossible to get a coffin into the ward and as a consequence the corpse had to be carried outside and then put in the coffin. This caused considerable inconvenience and danger to those dealing with the situation. His pregnant wife, along with a child and nurses, remained in the hospital until the doctor was satisfied that they were free from smallpox.[19]

Understandably, not everybody was happy about the fact that the hospital was situated near a cemetery, and at a council meeting the convener stated: "*You murder your patients by taking them there. They will look out on the graves and ask 'why have you brought us here to be buried?' It is a cruel place, a wretched place for the hospital.*"

Nobody could deny that this was so but, from the point of view of preventing the spread of contagious diseases, having a hospital near a cemetery meant that the corpse could be removed and quickly buried without having to be transported through a populous area.

The hospital had become too small by 1885 and the cost of extending was prohibitive. A committee was appointed to consider the feasibility of the local authorities of the burgh and landward district to combine to provide a suitable fever hospital for the parish on another site. Work was completed on the Lerwick Combination Hospital by June 1889, and consisted of 26 beds (on part of the site of the present Gilbert Bain Hospital). It was more commonly known as the Isolation Hospital and, in August 1889, the mate of a Danish smack suffering from typhoid fever was the first patient admitted there.[20]

The Fever Hospital at the Knab was in a somewhat dilapidated state when, in 1904, a wooden hut was erected behind the building to receive cases of smallpox. The following year a naval reserve sailor was admitted and was attended to by a man who had already had smallpox. The next day the matron of the Combination Hospital and her assistant (the hospital being empty at the time), volunteered to nurse the man, who recovered.[21]

The medical officer of health reported in 1929 that the smallpox isolation building at the Knab was now untenable and derelict.[22]

Smallpox was declared to be eradicated worldwide in 1980 following a global immunisation campaign led by the World Health Organization.[23]

17. *The hospital in a derelict state with the wooden hut built at the back in 1904 to receive smallpox patients. c.1910*

Twageos and Twageos House

18. *Twageos from the sea showing, from left: Jeannie Bult's Hoose, Strong's House, Twageos House, the Widows' Homes, The Knowe, Anderson Educational Institute, Lower and Upper Leog. Late 1880s*

In 1771 the village of Twageos, reputed to have received its name from the two geos that are in the vicinity (Old Norse *Gjá* – a cleft in the landscape), consisted of eight houses with kail yards and byres, a smithy, a booth and lofted warehouses, mill and mill-house, limekiln, pier, artificial beach for drying fish, and stone and slate quarries.[1] The village was eventually swallowed up to become part of Lerwick.

On the site of South Ness house stood Jeannie Bult's Hoose, a tenement which was derelict by the end of the 19th century. In 1871 Jane Bolt was recorded as a washerwoman, and three other families shared the house.[2] It is a general belief that she kept lodgers.[3] The walls were still standing when the site was cleared for the building of South Ness House in 1902 for Alexander Mitchell, bank agent, Union Bank (now Bank of Scotland).[4]

The house opposite was occupied by Mr Thomas Strong and his family who lived there for about 40 years from 1850. He was a boot and shoemaker who had a shop on the upper side of Commercial Street, which became Economy Corner in 1935.[5] (This was demolished in 1966 to make way for Church Road.) The house was later occupied by Mr Hyslop, for many years the gardener at Twageos House. It continued to be known as Hyslop's Cottage, despite later tenants residing there, until its demolition in the late 1950s to make way for the coastguard houses.

Today all these old buildings have long disappeared, including the somewhat imposing, mysterious and allegedly haunted Twageos House, which was situated near the bottom of the present Gressy Loan on the south side.

The exact date for the erection of Twageos House is unknown, but it was most probably built at the beginning of the 18th century by the Earl of Morton to house his

19. Twageos House with Janet Courtney Hostel in the background. 1950s

personnel.[6] A document dated 1712 refers to James Isaacson, chamberlain to the Earl of Morton.[7]

It was believed that the north part of the house was the oldest and had five rooms.[8] An extension was added about 1750 when it became the residence of William Chalmers, controller of customs and factor for the Earl of Morton. The second meeting of the newly created Morton Lodge met in Twageos House on 1st January, 1765.[9] He proceeded to buy the surrounding land and property but in 1766 he lost his position of factor when the islands were transferred by the Earl of Morton to Sir Laurence Dundas. In addition, Chalmers was discovered to have been engaged in smuggling, which resulted in his dismissal as controller of customs. He died in 1772 and a protracted legal dispute over his debts followed between his widow and Dundas.

At that time Mrs Chalmers and the family moved to what was known as Patrick Torrie's House (10 Commercial Street). For several years she collected a small rent from the tenants of Twageos, but ultimately lost possession to Dundas.[10] Twageos House was held in the Dundas family until about 1827 when it was sold to John Bruce of Sumburgh.[11]

Part of Twageos House was also the residence of the Rev. James Sands, who was the fourth parish minister, from 1767 to 1793.[12] The fifth parish minister, from 1793 to 1797, was the Rev. John Macleod and he also resided in Twageos.[13]

During the 19th century several families resided in this house. They included the Rev. John McKinven, Congregational minister, and his large family in the 1860s and Robert Mouat, general merchant, and family during the 1870s. They were followed by James K. Galloway, procurator fiscal and solicitor in the 1880s then Samuel Fordyce, plumber, with wife and family in the 1890s. At the turn of the century Twageos House was occupied by James C. Grierson, solicitor, and family.

A resident who lived there from the early years of the 20th century was Miss Christina Jamieson.[14] Around about 1925 she formed the Shetland Folk Lore Society, with emphasis on preserving old Shetland tunes, songs, stories and dances. She allowed members to meet in the kitchen where concerts and plays were rehearsed, stories were

20. *Papa Stour Sword Dancers at one of Miss Christina Jamieson's Shetland Folk Lore Society evenings in the grounds of Twageos House. c.1930*

relayed and tunes played. Film clips exist of the group dancing in the courtyard. These gatherings ended when Miss Jamieson joined her brother in New Zealand in 1935.[15]

The house was described in the 1930s as a sprawling building with ten rooms on three floors, with six feet thick walls and a cockloft running the full length. On the ground floor there was a parlour, a servant's room, and a large farmhouse kitchen with a low ceiling, flagged floor and large fireplace with the stumps remaining of what had been a turnspit. The drawing room and guest bedroom were on the first floor with dining room on the south side, and four bedrooms were on the top floor – two large rooms at each end and two small rooms in between – and a stairway to the cockloft.

Roofed passageways at the back linked the house to a dairy, peat store, toilet and wash-house from where water was pumped from a well under the flagged floor. Another well was situated in the narrow passage between the north wall and the gable of the house. A ten feet (3m) high garden wall surrounded the house, and entrance to the flagged courtyard was gained through an arched gateway with a heavy wooden door. At the other side there was a hay store, coach house and harness room, with the paddock beyond where there was a well near the wall which was used for watering cattle. The garden at the front stretched down to Twageos Road.[16]

Twageos House was reputed to be haunted. The occupants soon learned to ignore hearing knocking at the door, preceded by footsteps in the corridor, as invariably nobody would be there! The 'pin legged fiddler' was often heard. A noise, similar to someone with a halting, clumping walk, was followed by the

21. *Gressy Loan at the junction with Twageos Road. Twageos House is on the left. 1950s*

strains of the fiddle – sometimes a slow air, sometimes a lively spring. It is not known who this individual may have been.[17]

The system of bell pulls, which previously connected the various bedrooms, the drawing room and dining room to the kitchen, was long broken, or corroded, yet bells could be heard ringing on occasion. Items would disappear when one's back was turned. One winter's day the occupants heard the latch of the main gate being opened and the gate slamming shut, followed by loud hammering at the door. When opened no one was there, just footprints in the snow leading up to the door! Nobody was found to have entered the building, or departed by another exit, and another occupant who was in Twageos Road at the time heading for home saw no one in the vicinity.

Strange noises and happenings took place but no sighting of an apparition was ever reported, the exception being whatever a visitor's dog saw, or sensed, which frightened him so much that he stood growling with teeth bared in a passageway. He then turned tail and scratched at the door in a frantic effort to get outside, and then bolted for home.[18]

The Bruce estate became The Sumburgh Company Limited in 1907, on the death of John Bruce the Younger and the succession to Robert H. Bruce.[19] In 1935 the company sold land including Twageos House to Lerwick Town Council.[20]

The Henry family, the next occupants, kept guests until they moved to the Grand Hotel in 1950.[21] Twageos House was then used as temporary accommodation for many families and to young boys the ancient, mysterious and sprawling building, including the large loft, was a fascinating place in which to explore and play.[22]

In 1958 the Ministry of Works acquired land from Lerwick Town Council for the erection of a new Coastguard Station and related housing. This transfer included a large garden, three lock-up garages and Twageos House, which by this time was in very poor condition.[23] However, the council was given permission to continue to use the building to provide temporary housing until the decision was made, by the Ministry of Works, to either use or demolish Twageos House.[24]

The last occupant was Mr John Fraser, who originated from Papa Stour, a somewhat eccentric old man who was an avid fiddler. He resisted eviction by barricading himself in, but to no avail. The destruction of the house took place in 1961. It was said that woodworm beetles invaded neighbouring houses following the removal of the roof.[25]

Although Twageos House was in poor condition at the time, it now seems incredible that a decision was made to demolish such an historic old building, part of which had stood for over 250 years. In doing so an important aspect of our heritage was lost forever.

22. *Twageos House under demolition and work commencing on the Coastguard Houses. February 1961*

Gressy Loan and Surrounding Area

23. *The Knab and cemetery, to the right is Gressy Loan leading down to the Coastguard Houses with South Ness House in the foreground. Late 1962*

When you hear older folk tell how they sledged down Gressy Loan when they were bairns, what immediately springs to mind is how dangerous it could have been. However, the Gressy Loan they are referring to is not the steep, wide road linking Twageos Road to Knab Road we are familiar with today, but the grassy track with the bend shown on the right of the photograph taken in 1962. When the private houses in Gressy Loan were built about 1967 the track was straightened and later tarmacadamed.[1]

The newly built Coastguard Houses[2] are shown at the junction of Twageos Road and Gressy Loan. Immediately behind the houses is the site of Twageos House, and part remaining wall of its wash-house. The earliest part of the large imposing house had stood from before 1712 until its demolition in 1961.

The local authority houses on the lower right, at the bottom of Gressy Loan, were part of the Twageos Road housing scheme, first occupied in 1936.

The small rectangular shape directly opposite the foot of the Loan was all that remained of the Second World War Twageos Camp. It consisted of several Nissen huts, including a large lecture room/training hall used for air gunners' training in aircraft recognition, as well as the nearby sergeants' mess, and accommodation for the men.

Due to severe shortage of housing after the war, some returning servicemen with their families squatted in the lower huts for a time until they were offered alternative accommodation. These huts were then demolished.[3]

The Army had allowed the nearby residents the use of the lecture room/training hall during the Victory in Europe gala day celebration in May 1945.[4] A bonfire with an effigy of Goering was set alight and fireworks were set off while it burned. Everyone then returned to the hut for refreshments.[5]

This hut, along with the adjacent former sergeants' mess, was retained and became a Social Club for the Twageos folk. The much-used hut was the venue for dances, concerts, Christmas parties, film shows, etc., badminton and the Ladies Guild. It was an Up-Helly-A' hall for five years from 1949 and the smaller hut was used as the supper room and as a tearoom for other social events. Sadly, the Social Club came to a sudden and unexpected end on 31st January 1953 when the hut was damaged beyond repair in the violent storm that struck the UK.[6]

South Ness House is surrounded by a wall and was built in 1902 for Alexander Mitchell, who was the Manager of the Union Bank (now Bank of Scotland). In 1924 the Education Authority purchased the house[7]. In 1962 Mr Bill Rhind, rector of the Anderson Educational Institute, and his family were the occupants.

Many changes have occurred over the years since the photograph on the previous page was taken but when walking around the Knab it is not immediately apparent that many Second World War structures still remain.

The small building to the left of the Coastguard Houses was an engine room and control point for the guns during the war. It was camouflaged to resemble a cottage, by having a thatched roof and painted-on windows. In 1962 it was being used to garage a Lerwick Town Council truck.[8]

Behind the South Ness Light, and to the left of South Ness House, was a gun

24. *Twageos Camp with South Ness House in the background. The lecture room/training hall, later used as the Twageos Social Club, is the hut on the right. 1940s*

placement (now built over). The No. 2 and 3 searchlight emplacement can be seen next to the Light and further along the footpath, below the bend, is searchlight emplacement No. 1.

Twageos Road leads on to the Knab footpath. Below the cemetery is the old quarry from where stones were taken to build many of the old houses in Lerwick, including Fort Charlotte in 1781. Also visible is the fixed torpedo tube platform, established as part of Lerwick harbour defences.

The footpath then leads to the point of the Knab, with the Horse's Head on the left and watch huts, observation points, No. 2 gun placement and magazine on the right. A dry-stone dyke currently surrounds the site of No. 1 gun placement at the upper end of Knab Road.[9]

Along Knab Road, beyond the cemetery and to the right of the top of Gressy Loan is what was referred to as the Knab Camp, but was officially part of HMS Fox naval base. After the war these wooden huts provided temporary housing for servicemen and their families, some of whom also squatted.

By 1968 most of the huts had been sold and removed but the last occupants were not housed until March 1970.[10]

Many people have fond memories of the original Gressy Loan, Knab Camp, Twageos House and the Social Club.

25. *Celebrating Victory in Europe with the effigy of Goering on top of the bonfire. May 1945. Back row from left: Maggie Winchester, Nancy Pearson, Mary Robertson, Celie Coutts, Ewen Coutts, Jenny Robertson, Judy Winchester, Eunice Paton, Zegena Robertson, John Johnston, Bertha Henderson, Alice Sutherland and unknown. Third row from left: Sheila Wright, Rene Winchester, Pat Reade, Grace Henderson, Marlene Henderson, Jesma Johnston and Isobel Sinclair. Second row from left: Beth Coutts, Beryl Lawrence, Rosie Lawrence, Bobbie Gallie, Patricia Farmer, Peter Farmer and Margaret Johnston. Front row from left: Gordon Farmer, George Irvine, Billy Wright, Arthur Sinclair, Leslie Angus, Douglas Sinclair (not the author), James Winchester, Ian Sinclair, Morris Pearson and Ian McAlpine.*

26. *Lieut. John Reade of the Pioneer Corps and his wife Joan outside South Ness House. He helped organise the Victory in Europe Gala Day. Mrs Reade was a Shetlander and her sister Margaret and brother-in-law, George Irvine, lived in Twageos Road. 1945*

Relics of Wartime

27.

This photograph of the Twageos area, taken in 1962, shows remaining wartime buildings and the early stages of the building of the extension to the Anderson Educational Institute (AEI) which had opened on 4th August, 1862.[1]

In 1970 the Institute, as it was commonly known, became the Anderson High School.[2] An open weekend was held at the school on 6th and 7th October, 2012, to celebrate the 150th anniversary.[3]

The temporary classrooms in front of the AEI were remnants of the Second World War, when the military requisitioned the Institute for use as a military hospital and pupils had to double up at Lerwick Central Public School.[4]

The T-shaped building, the domestic science hut, was used at Up-Helly-A' to provide supper from 1954 until the early 1960s. The smaller of the two lower buildings, the gymnasium, was used by the Twageos Social Club, and at Up-Helly-A' for dancing, while the lower woodwork/technical drawing hut was utilised as a waiting room for guizers.[5]

The buildings shown top left form the Knab Camp, part of the wartime naval base known as HMS Fox. After the war the huts were converted for family use and provided rented accommodation until March 1970.[6]

Adjacent to the Knab Camp, on the cleared ground to the rear of the AEI, was the site of the Bellevue Camp. Nissen and wooden huts had been erected there during the war for use by the RAF.[7]

The Janet Courtney Hostel, to the left of the Institute, was under construction when the Second World War broke out.[8] The main structure was sufficiently complete to make it useful for RAF Fighter Operations HQ and all warnings of approaching enemy aircraft emanated from there. Early in the hostilities the basement was used as an air-raid shelter for AEI pupils. After the war the building was completed and it reverted to its original purpose as a hostel for school boys.[9] It was officially opened in October 1947.[10]

To the right of the AEI was the Bruce Hostel for school girls, gifted by Robert H. Bruce of Sumburgh and Lunna. The First World War delayed construction but it was finally opened in 1923. For a short time at the beginning of the Second World War it was requisitioned and occupied by the admiral of the fleet, the Earl of Cork and Orrery, and his staff.[11] The building now houses the Bruce Family Centre Services.

The huts (near bottom right) were also part of the HMS Fox naval base and were occupied by Wrens (Women's Royal Naval Service). In 1947 these became the Midgarth Maternity Annexe where nearly a generation of Shetlanders were born until the Maternity Unit opened in the former Isolation Block, New Gilbert Bain Hospital, in 1962.[12] A part of HMS Fox, namely the weather vane in the shape of a fox, was removed from the Knab Camp site and could be seen until recently on the roof of a building at Hay & Company Buildbase, Freefield.[13]

Twageos Road is in the foreground. Near the junction of the road with Lovers Loan stands Midgarth House, built in 1906 for John William Laurenson, woollen draper and hosier.[14]

28. *The Midgarth Maternity Annexe*

The Hostels – A Brief History

29. *The Bruce Hostel*

The Bruce Hostel

Prior to hostels being built in Lerwick, country pupils attending for secondary education at the Anderson Educational Institute (later Anderson High School) had to find lodgings in the town, often sharing a house with adult workers. As this was not an ideal situation the provision of purpose-built accommodation was considered necessary.[1]

Mr Robert H. Bruce of Sumburgh and Lunna, although living in London, had long intended to make a gift to Shetland. He donated a site at Twageos and funded the building of a hostel for girl boarders near 'da Institute'.[2]

Mr W. L. MacDougall, estate agent, Sumburgh, drew the plan to accommodate 44 boarders, and the contractor was the well-known local master builder Mr John M. Aitken. Work commenced in 1914 only to be seriously delayed by the advent of the First World War.

With a magnificent view overlooking Lerwick Harbour, the Bruce Hostel is a very impressive building. A broad flight of steps, in Sumburgh stone, leads to the terrace and the imposing entrance. The main front is Eday freestone and is supported by two massive freestone columns. Above the door is the Bruce arms and motto "*Omnia vincit amor*" and 1919.

On 9th August, 1923, the hostel was opened by Dr MacDonald, Secretary of the Scottish Educational Department. Girls moved in on 27th August but, sadly, Mr Aitken died on the same day. The first matron was Miss Elizabeth Anderson from Callander, who was chosen from 103 applicants.

Mr John Wingate, Robert Bruce's nephew, donated a large bronze vase in 1936 which was placed in the hall.[3]

In 1939 Britain was again at war. Provision of additional hospital accommodation for service personnel and civilians was deemed necessary. Mr Daniel Lamont, surgeon at Gilbert Bain Memorial Hospital (now Goudies Funeral Directors Ltd), identified Bruce Hostel as an ideal auxiliary hospital. However, no sooner had preliminary arrangements been made when, in July 1940, plans were thwarted by the arrival of the admiral of the fleet, the Earl of Cork and Orrery, who had been detailed to Shetland to assume command of the islands and to prepare for a possible invasion.

On entering Lerwick Harbour the somewhat flamboyant admiral saw the Bruce Hostel, and despite protest from Mr Lamont, claimed it for his headquarters.[4] The stay however was short lived, as by November the threat of invasion was considered to be unlikely and the admiral was sent to Gibraltar[5] and on the 30th of that month the hostel reopened. In the meantime a hutted emergency hospital was constructed near the Tingwall manse.[6]

In 1942 the AEI was taken over by the army as a military hospital and pupils were evacuated to Lerwick Central Public School until April 1946.[7]

In the 1950s the rules for Bruce Hostel were rather draconian based on today's standards. Girls were expected to rise at 7.30am, with prayers at 8.05am. Following evening tea, study was from 6.00 to 9.00pm with supper at 9.15pm. They retired at 9.50pm and 'lights out' was at 10.15pm, with no noise thereafter. Attendance at church on Sunday was compulsory.[8] During the war years it was strictly forbidden for girls to talk to the soldiers stationed in the neighbouring army camp.[9]

30. *The Janet Courtney Hostel*

The Janet Courtney Hostel

Although the girls' hostel had opened in 1923 it was to be another 15 years before work commenced on a boys' hostel, following a request by the Zetland County Council Education Committee to the Carnegie United Kingdom Trust – established by Andrew Carnegie, the Scots-American philanthropist, in 1913.[10]

Work started in 1938 but was disrupted by war. As mentioned in the previous chapter, the main structure was sufficiently complete to make it useful for RAF Fighter Operations HQ with all warnings of approaching enemy aircraft emanating from there.[11] Early in the war the basement was used as an air-raid shelter for AEI pupils. Sometimes one of the boys played an accordion and an impromptu dance followed.

The building was released in autumn 1945 and building work recommenced the following spring. The cost was met by the Trust with the exception of £3,000 from the Zetland County Council Education Committee for furnishings and £2,000 compensation received for requisitioning.

The builder was Messrs Wm. Dale & Sons Ltd, Dunfermline, and Fram Reinforcing Concrete Company of Glasgow was responsible for the ferro-concrete construction. Sixteen other contractors were involved but no Shetland firm was engaged on the work.

The hostel was built on a dressed stone foundation with harled brick walls and could accommodate 40 boys.

A bronze plaque at the front door stated: "*This building, the gift of the Carnegie United Kingdom Trustees, was opened in October 1947 and named the Janet Courtney Hostel in token of Mrs Courtney's continuous service as a member of the Trust since its foundation in 1913.*"

The opening ceremony took place in the study where 60 guests gathered in the company of Sir Basil Neven-Spence MP, Mr E. Salter Davies CBE, chairman of the Carnegie UK Trustees, and Lieutenant Colonel Magnus Shearer OBE TD. An elderly

Mrs Courtney was unfortunately unable to undertake the long journey to Shetland. Mr Davies handed the Hostel over to Lieutenant Colonel Shearer who was representing Zetland Education Authority.

Staff consisted of Miss Elsie B. Hay, matron, Mr J. R. S. Clark MA, housemaster, as well as four maids and a cook.

As the guests were departing one of the first boys to arrive, carrying his suitcase, was Peter Tait of Aywick, East Yell.[12]

HOUSE OF CHARITY

Remarkably, Westminster Abbey and St Magnus Scottish Episcopal Church at Greenfield have something in common, namely stained glass windows designed by Sir Ninian Comper. Born in Aberdeen in 1864, he is described as one of the last great Gothic Revival architects who specialised almost entirely in churches and their contents. Throughout his long life he refused accolades and it was with great reluctance that he accepted a knighthood in 1950 in recognition of his work. He had been proposed by John Betjeman. Sir Ninian designed churches throughout the world and so famous was he that, following his death in 1960, his ashes were buried in the north aisle, Westminster Abbey, near a series of windows designed by him.[1]

The original location of his windows in Lerwick was not in St Magnus Church but in the building still referred to as the 'House of Charity' in Knab Road. It was built in 1904 from designs by Mr J. M. Aitken, local architect and contractor, and is now part of Glen Orchy House.[2]

The House of Charity, officially St Magnus Home but seldom referred to by its correct title, was erected in the grounds of Annsbrae House as a memorial to Mrs Mary Margaret Cameron, wife of Major Thomas Mouat Cameron of the Garth and Annsbrae estates, who had died on 17th January of that year.

Before returning to Shetland to reside in the houses of Gardie and Annsbrae, she had lived in India with her husband, who had served in the 55th Regiment of the Bengal Native Infantry. They were there during the 1857 Indian Mutiny.[3]

The Cameron family had close connections with St Magnus Church as Mrs Cameron was actually one of the founders, along with her husband who had donated the site. The foundation stone was laid on St Magnus Day, 16th April, 1863, and the church was completed and consecrated on 27th June, 1864. The tower was added in 1891.[4] She had helped in the revival of Episcopal faith in the islands after an absence of about 100 years. When the major died in December 1892 he was buried in a vault under the altar of the church. Mrs Cameron was laid to rest with him in 1904. A memorial plaque marks the location.[5]

31. *The House of Charity, Knab Road. 1960*

32. St Magnus Scottish Episcopal Church. c.1904

Mrs Cameron had taken a keen interest in the welfare of the people of Lerwick. She was the instigator of the Lerwick Sick Aid Society in 1896 and was elected its president that same year. The society was affiliated with Queen Victoria's Jubilee Institute for Nurses, with one of its objects being the "Nursing of the Sick Poor in their own homes".[6] The institute was a precursor of district nurse training.

It had been Mrs Cameron's desire to have Christian Sisters based in Lerwick who would live for others, and work among the people and care and comfort them in their time of need.

Following Mrs Cameron's death, her son and two daughters carried out her wishes and, on 7th February, 1904, work commenced on building the House of Charity. The memorial stone, with the inscription *"To the Glory of God and in thankful remembrance of His servant Mary Margaret Cameron, this House of Charity is dedicated 1904"*, was laid and dedicated by the Bishop of the United Diocese of Aberdeen and Orkney on 16th June. It was placed in the east gable using a mallet made of wood from the Gardie garden.[7]

The House of Charity opened on 27th December, 1904, and the small private Chapel of the Holy Spirit was blessed.[8] A sale of work had been held in the premises two weeks earlier to raise funds for completing the furnishing and fittings.[9]

The entrance was through a glass porch and there were two classrooms, one smaller than the other, a sitting room, dining room, kitchen and scullery. Upstairs was the chapel, three bedrooms providing accommodation for the Sisters, servants' room and box room with a large loft above.[10]

The Comper stained glass windows consisted of triple windows in the chapel overlooking Knab Road, which were dedicated in memory of Mrs Cameron on 26th June, 1905, by the Bishop,[11] and a pair of windows in the south wall in memory of Lt. James W. Pochin RN, a lay preacher in St Magnus Church. He had arrived in Lerwick in 1901 to take up the post of battery divisional officer of HM Coastguard at Fort Charlotte. He enjoyed shooting and fishing. During a shooting trip to Girlsta Loch he did not return and was last seen there on 19th October, 1904. Although searches were undertaken his body was not found until 3rd December. It is presumed he had drowned, despite being a strong swimmer, but the circumstances surrounding his death are not known. His burial took place in Berkshire but a small memorial was erected the following year beside the loch on the west side at the spot where some belongings were found. He was 42 years old.[12]

33. Memorial to Lt. James W. Pochin, beside the Girlsta Loch. 2013

The connection with Ninian Comper had come about because his father, the Rev. John Comper, had persuaded the Sisters of the Society of St Margaret, at East Grinstead, to establish a community in Aberdeen, and he became the rector of St Margaret of Scotland in Aberdeen. The mother superior was none other than the Major and Mrs Cameron's daughter, Mother Margaret Anne, hence the connection with the House of Charity. She had been involved with the planning of the house and was instrumental in sending to Lerwick the Sisters of St Margaret, or St Margaret's Sisterhood.[13]

Two sisters arrived in 1902: Annie Stevenson and for a short time Miss Gutteres. They lived in private accommodation until the house was ready for occupancy.[14]

Sister Christine Mary and Sister Ethel are mentioned too, but it was Harriette Lendrum[15] who accompanied Sister Annie for over ten years.

Local people who remembered the Sisters of Mercy, and in particular Sister Annie, told that they wore nuns' habit and were well known around the town. During the summer months they tended to the needs of the numerous herring workers based at the north end of Lerwick.

In those pre-NHS days there were many Lerwegians who could not afford to pay for treatment at the Gilbert Bain Memorial Hospital (now Goudie's Funeral Directors), and the sisters nursed and cared for them in their own homes. It was said that many people became Episcopalians due to the example shown by Sister Annie.[16]

The nuns left in 1919, when elderly Sister Annie and Sister Harriette were withdrawn and there were no younger sisters available to replace them.[17]

The House of Charity then became the rectory for St Magnus Church (not to be confused with the present rectory situated near the church). The Sunday school and Girls Guild met there, and once a month a service was held in the chapel for the Girls Guild.

The house underwent considerable repairs and reconstruction in 1939 and it would seem that the chapel was rededicated to Sisters Mary and Margaret. It was described

34. The twin windows in memory of Lt. James W. Pochin, now in St Magnus Church. 2013

35. The Signature of the Strawberry incorporated into the Pochin window above left. 2013

as being pretty, with the stained glass windows, whitewashed walls and wooden seating. Many local couples were married in the chapel.[18]

The rectory had a number of spare rooms and these were let to lodgers. During the Second World War, army officers were billeted there and their wives held sewing sessions at which local girls were taught the skill. It became a popular place for the church's choirboys, who were attracted by the constant offer of good food made available by the housekeeper Miss White. The army no doubt supplied the extra rations.[19]

In 1969 the building was no longer required and was sold into private ownership,[20] then to Mr W. Miller in 1971, but not before the Comper windows were removed to St Magnus Church for storage. In 1972 the Rev. Derek Wallace instigated the removal of the clear windows in the church and had them replaced with the windows from the House of Charity which had been sent to Bristol for restoration and alteration. The windows were rededicated on 28th October, 1973.[21]

The triple windows, which were originally in the chapel, are now three separate windows. The one depicting the Blessed Virgin Mary is on the left from the entrance while those of St John the Evangelist and St Margaret of Scotland are on the opposite side, as are the two 'Pochin' windows.

There is no doubt that these are Sir Ninian Comper windows because, if one looks carefully, his distinguishing mark, the Signature of the Strawberry, can be found on both sets. He incorporated a strawberry into his work after 1903, as a tribute to his father who died that year in Duthie Park, Aberdeen, while distributing strawberries to the poor. These windows are therefore among the first to have the strawberry signature.

Glen Orchy House changed hands in 1991 and following extensive refurbishment and additions it became the guesthouse we see today.

MISSIONS TO SEAMEN INSTITUTE
(THE FLYING ANGEL)

In 1835 John Ashley, an Anglican priest, started visiting ships at anchor in the Bristol Channel. He found that the crews had no contact with any church, and was so moved by their isolation and need that he decided to devote his life to serving them. He built a cutter named *Eirene*, which had a chapel below decks, and visited ships at anchor in the Channel. In 15 years he visited 14,000 ships and sold more than 5,000 bibles and prayer books to seamen.

John Ashley's work inspired Anglican ministries in other ports and it was decided, in 1856, that there should be one organisation to co-ordinate and expand this ministry to seafarers. It was called the Missions to Seamen and in 1858 it adopted an angel as its sign, inspired by a verse from the book of Revelation, Chapter 14: "*And I saw another angel fly in the midst of Heaven, having the everlasting Gospel to preach unto them that dwell on earth, and to every nation, and kindred, and tongue, and people.*"

Initially the Missions to Seamen, as a missionary society of the Anglican Church, cared for Britain's extensive merchant fleet seafarers, providing reading rooms, health and religious education, and assistance. As the shipping industry became more international, drawing its crews from different countries, the Mission extended its care to all seafarers whatever their nationality or creed.[1] (The Missions to Seamen should not be confused with the Royal National Mission to Deep Sea Fishermen, whose interest in Shetland dates from 1891 when a Mission smack visited the fishing fleets operating around the islands.)[2]

During 1920, at the urgent request of the Fisherfolk committee of the Representative Church Council of the Episcopal Church in Scotland, the Missions to Seamen developed a new branch of its activities, namely to work amongst the fisher-girls at Lerwick, and Miss Mary Grahame was sent to Shetland in May. Although the herring fishing lasted for only four to five months each year, the huge influx of fishermen and fish workers arriving in May put a severe strain on Lerwick's recreational and first aid facilities. The women and girls employed to gut the fish had to work for long hours in the open in all weathers, with their fingers rough and reddened from constant contact with salt. A careless moment when tired meant another cut that was slow to heal in spite of the thick swathes of bandages applied for protection. It fell to local churches to

36. *The Missions to Seamen 'Flying Angel' sign*

37. *The interior of St Michael's Mission Hall which opened in 1902 at Grantfield*

provide appropriate facilities through the establishment of rest huts, staffed with nurses.

On her arrival in Lerwick, Miss Grahame set about getting accommodation for the exclusive use of the girls.[3] St Magnus Scottish Episcopal Church obtained a large redundant hut which had been brought to Lerwick and erected at Alexandra Wharf as a canteen for naval personnel stationed there. When the base closed in 1919, Lerwick Harbour Trust requested that the hut be removed as the site was required. However, the Missions to Seamen had use of the hut for almost a year until it was relocated on the upper side of the North Road near Holmsgarth.[4] The Church Army hut was purchased by the Salvation Army.

During this time the Mission to Seamen also had use of St Michael's Mission Hall, which was rented from St Magnus Scottish Episcopal Church. The small wooden building, consisting of a small church and two classrooms, had opened at Grantfield in 1902 on what is now part of the site of the Salvation Army building, to serve the fishing community who lived there. It was used during the fishing season as a reading room and dispensary where the Mission's nurse tended to the fish workers' hands.

In a very short time the hut and canteen at Holmsgarth was used by a considerable number of girls. Games, concerts and knitting competitions formed a pleasant change for those who had been working long hours over the gutting farlins.

Mission workers sent from London and Aberdeen provided help, as did the district nurse, who treated over 200 cases of cut or poisoned hands during the 1920 season when a total of 2,748 girls used the facilities. The distance from the centre of Lerwick, and the pressure of work in connection with St Magnus Church, precluded the rector of Lerwick (who was the Missions to Seamen chaplain) from paying more than a very occasional visit either to St Michael's or to the recreation hut. Miss Grahame frequently took prayers in the premises.[5]

In 1921 the hut was let as a labour bureau. Within a fortnight a serious fire completely destroyed it and all the paper and documents connected with the unemployed of Shetland were lost. At the time there was a strong rumour that the fire was deliberate.

From insurance money a new hut was erected on the site and the good work continued.[6]

The Missions to Seamen obtained a piece of ground in Charlotte Street from the North Star Cinema Co[7] on which was built a mission hall and house for the caretaker. During 1926 the Mission was opened in November by Sir W. Watson Cheyne, Bart., Lord Lieutenant of the county. It was the fourth station to be opened in Scotland.[8] The following year the trustees of the Bishop of Aberdeen's Diocesan Fund became the proprietors.[9]

In 1938 a chapel – the Seamen's Church of St Peter – was created in the Charlotte Street mission. Services had continued to be held at St Michael's Mission Hall at Grantfield until then, when it was let and later sold to the Salvation Army.[10]

In 1953 the trustees of the Bishop of Aberdeen's Diocesan Fund sold the Charlotte Street building to the Missions to Seamen.[11] Here, in what was commonly known as the Flying Angel mission, short services were held for seafarers on Sunday evenings as well as prayers commencing at 10.00am and 9.30pm during the week, with Holy Communion on request from the rector of St Magnus Church.

Recreation facilities included snooker, billiards, table tennis, reading and writing conveniences and canteen facilities for light refreshments.[12]

38. In 1938 the Seamen's Church of St Peter was created in the Charlotte Street Mission Hall (now Havly)

When the Flying Angel closed in 1958, the building was acquired by the Norwegian Department of Fisheries and operated as the Norwegian Welfare Centre. At that time large numbers of Norwegian vessels were fishing in Shetland waters. There were several officers in charge until 1973, when Mr Reidar Vetvik, his wife Astrid and their family relocated from Norway.

In 1979 a separate Norwegian organisation, Den Indre Sjømannsmisjon, or the Home Mission to Seamen, opened Havly (a shelter from the sea) in the Shetland News' former printworks in Mounthooly Street. Church services were held in Havly each Sunday but when the last of its three missionaries left in March 1985, and was not replaced, Mr and Mrs Vetvik were asked to look after Havly in addition to the welfare centre.

39. The Norwegian Welfare Centre, Charlotte Street. 1960s

40. Sjømannstua Havly in Mounthooly Street. Late 1980s

On 1st December, 1991, the Norwegian Department of Fisheries decided to close its welfare centres throughout the world. The Norwegian Home Mission to Seamen bought the centre in Charlotte Street and it became the new Havly, with combined secular and religious functions.

Large numbers of Scandinavian visitors called at the Havly during the summer months, including the crews of yachts who could use the telephone and facilities provided for showers and laundry. Reidar and Astrid acted as interpreters in all the Scandinavian languages and frequently assisted the coastguard, police, the sheriff court, doctors and the Gilbert Bain Hospital when dealing with visiting seamen.

The entire building was refurbished in 1993 and Havly reopened on 23rd August, providing facilities for seafarers and a meeting place for local organisations, prayer and support groups. A church service was held every Sunday morning. Tourism was promoted and Havly advertised as the only cafe in Shetland offering genuine Norwegian coffee, cakes, waffles, snacks and open sandwiches, becoming a favourite place with locals.[13]

The establishment became a privately owned cafe in 2010 and, following refurbishment, lost its Norwegian style interior and charm, but the three arched windows of the Seamen's Church of St Peter can still be seen there.

Mr and Mrs Vetvik continued to live in their Mounthooly Street home until they moved back to Norway in 2016.

41. Reidar and Astrid Vetvik

ARTHUR ANDERSON AND CRUISING

The number of cruise ships visiting Lerwick has increased greatly in recent years. On Sunday 2nd August, 2009, the *MV Boudicca* was the 1,000th ship since records began in 1924 to arrive in port.[1]

The first entry for cruise ships recorded by Lerwick Harbour Trust (now Lerwick Port Authority), was on 17th July, 1928, when the *Mira* arrived from Kirkwall carrying 112 members of the Old Norse Society of Bergen, Norway.[2] However, as far back as 1886, the North of Scotland and Orkney and Shetland Steam Navigation Company Ltd introduced cruises to the Norwegian fjords by the *St Rognvald I*, calling along Lerwick on her return journey. Over the period 1886-1908 the *St Sunniva I*, which was built for cruising, also carried tourists to the North Cape, Baltic and Mediterranean.[3]

It may be surprising to learn that the inventor of cruising is believed to be none other than Arthur Anderson, who was born in the Böd of Gremista, Lerwick on 19th February, 1792.[4]

The advice given to the one time 'beach boy' on leaving Shetland was "*Dö weel and persevere*" – he rose to become a clerk to London shipbroker Brodie McGhie Willcox. In 1825 they formed a partnership trading as Willcox & Anderson. The firm began the

42. *Arthur Anderson from a portrait painted in 1850*

43. *The Böd of Gremista in 1953. It was uninhabited from 1948 until restored and opened as a museum by P&O Chairman Sir Jeffrey Sterling in 1987. It now houses the Shetland Textile Museum*

Peninsular Steam Company in 1834. In 1840 Oriental was added to the title and the company became the Peninsular & Oriental Steam Navigation Company, known as P&O.[5] Arthur Anderson was the managing director and chairman.

In 1835 Anderson created and published a newspaper, the *Shetland Journal*, to inform his fellow-islanders of world events. To fill an empty space in the first edition he put in a bogus sample advertisement. It announced that a mythical steam packet, the 'Hyperborean', under the command of Captain Magnus Turvalson, would provide travellers with the opportunity to cruise along the wild, west coast of Shetland, ascend Ronas Hill, then make the round voyage to the Faroe Islands and Iceland before returning to Scalloway.[6] It was surely carrying optimism too far if he hoped to find tourists brave enough to undertake that voyage in the North Atlantic, even in summer. Nine years later, cruising became a reality when P&O took up the idea – but to the Mediterranean, rather than the North Atlantic.

By 1844 there were a number of branch lines that connected with the company's regular mail ships to Alexandria, and it started to offer round-tickets to Malta, Athens, Smyrna, Constantinople (now Istanbul), Rhodes, Jaffa and Egypt and back to England, with shore excursions at each port of call.[7]

The government entered into a contract on 1st January, 1845, with the company to undertake to convey the mails from Suez to Ceylon (now Sri Lanka), and then northwards to Madras and Calcutta (now Chennai and Kolkata respectively), and eastwards to Penang, Singapore and Hong Kong.[8] The Mediterranean routes were abandoned but were revisited when cruising began in earnest after 1904.

Before 1854, P&O passengers to India could travel by the long route to Calcutta on the east coast or wait at Suez or Aden for an East Indian Company to Bombay (now Mombai). When the Bombay route passed to P&O it gave them a near monopoly of steamers east of Suez. In those days first class passengers were in the majority, with roughly two first class passengers to one second class. Most of the second class passengers were the first class passengers' servants, i.e. the batmen of the army officers, the maids of the memsahibs, and the Indian ayahs (nurse-maids) who looked after the children. Also travelling second class were low paid clergymen and missionaries.[9]

44. *Anderson Educational Institute. c.1904*

It has been suggested that the word 'posh' had its origin in the snobbishness of P&O's first class passengers, although etymologists deny it. When travelling to India through the Red Sea and Indian Ocean it was advantageous to have a north facing cabin, as it was much cooler. Soon people of importance demanded cabins 'Port Outward bound and Starboard Home'. Tickets were marked POSH and a new word was born.[10]

Arthur Anderson never forgot his humble start in life and maintained a close involvement with Shetland. He remembered the advice given to him and, in 1837, he founded the Shetland Fishery Company on Vaila in an effort to improve the plight of fishermen. He also introduced Shetland knitwear to a larger audience, including Queen Victoria. From 1847 until 1852, he was MP for Orkney and Shetland. In 1852 he opened a school in Skerries, then in 1862 the much larger Anderson Educational Institute (renamed Anderson High School in 1970). On the headland opposite the foot of Lovers Loan he established, in 1865, a Widows' Asylum (commonly referred to as Widows' Homes and renamed the Anderson Homes in 1971). The building was erected in memory of his wife, Mary Ann Hill, whom he had married in 1822, and it was intended for the widows of Shetland fishermen and sailors.[11]

Arthur Anderson died in London in 1868.[12] However, the advice "Dö weel and persevere", given in 1808 to the young Anderson by his employer Thomas Bolt, continues to this day as the Anderson High School motto.

On 3rd August, 1931, the luxury P&O liner *Viceroy of India* arrived in Lerwick harbour. This was her first port of call on a 21-day cruise to Norway and the northern capitals and was her third and last cruise of the season to Shetland.[13]

She was the company's most successful single vessel of the decade, having first come into service in 1929. For P&O the *Viceroy* was a model ship. Just under 20,000 gross tonnage she was powered by turbo-electric drive. This had been a relatively untried novelty, steam turbines powering electric motors, 17,000 horsepower producing 19 knots more smoothly and more quietly than ever before. In addition, the *Viceroy of India* had brought the traditional P&O liner to new levels of magnificent opulence and comfort. The first-class smoking room resembled, unbelievably, the great hall of a castle with hammer-beams, crossed swords decorating the walls, a large fireplace with baronial arms above it, comfortable armchairs, rugs and tables. Not surprisingly the *Viceroy* was immensely popular, with her '18th-century' music room, the dining saloon

45. *The Widows' Homes, now Anderson Homes, as viewed from the shore. c.1904*

46. P&O liner Viceroy of India in Lerwick Harbour. 1931

with its blue marbled pillars, an Adam-style reading room and the indoor swimming pool – P&O's first – surrounded by Pompeiian reliefs.[14]

The interest generated on this occasion by the liner's visit to Lerwick was partly because the co-founder of P&O was a Shetlander, but also from the fact that among the passengers was ex-King Alfonso of Spain, travelling as the Duke of Toledo, and accompanied by the Duke of Miranda.

The Duke of Toledo came ashore at about one o'clock to be met by Major A. Stephen, agent at Lerwick, who had arranged for the ex-King to visit Jarlshof. Mr A. O. Curle, who was in charge of excavations, showed him over the site. On return to Lerwick the Duke was taken, by his request, to the Shetland Hosiery Company shop (now the Commercial Street part of M&Co), where he purchased Shetland knitwear.

In the meantime, passengers had taken advantage of motor tours organised by Messrs Ganson Bros Ltd acting for Messrs Thomas Cook. (Ganson Bros Ltd was located in Harbour Street/Market Street, now the site of Market House.) Others had elected to spend their time shopping, with knitwear being the most popular purchase. Meanwhile, some of the crew did a brisk trade selling imitation pearl necklaces to local people.

Before the liner sailed at 4.30pm a crowd of spectators, some with cameras, gathered along the Esplanade. Others on board the *St Magnus*, lying alongside Victoria Pier, joined in to give the Duke a rousing farewell as he entered the launch to go off to the *Viceroy*.[15]

Unfortunately the *Viceroy of India*'s cruising days came to an end when she was requisitioned as a troopship and was torpedoed off North Africa on 11th November, 1942.[16]

Local people are still interested in visiting cruise ships. Many spectators are to be found at the Knab every summer admiring and taking photographs of increasingly larger ships such as the *Costa Pacifica* (114,500 gross tonnes with the capacity for carrying 3,780 passengers and 1,100 crew) and the *Celebrity Silhouette* (122,210 gross tonnes with the capacity for carrying 2,886 passengers). This is in stark contrast to the *Viceroy of India* at 19,645 gross tonnes.

THE KNOWE

47. *The Knowe with the Duke's Neb rock formation on the left. 1989*

In 1909 the well-known and highly respected boat builder Walter Duncan Snr, from Burra Isle, constructed a sixareen for use as a fishing/mail boat to run between Walls and the island of Foula.[1] Named the *Advance*, her first skipper was Magnus Manson who had been skipper of the previous mail boat.[2] Incredibly, the following year, at the age of 81, he emigrated to Australia![3] Laurence Gray replaced him. In 1912 an engine was fitted, and the *Advance* carried on the dual role until 1924 when she was no longer used for fishing. She was then heightened and, in 1937, a wheelhouse was erected aft.

The *Advance* served the Foula community as a mail boat for 40 years, until 1949, when she was beached at Ham for the final time and languished there until almost 30 years later, when local photographer Dennis Coutts found her. He decided that she would make a perfect roof for a garage, which he intended to build adjacent to his recently purchased house at The Knowe, opposite Leog, Lerwick.

The old mail boat clearly showed the ravages of time, but some remedial work by Dennis's brother Ian enabled her to be floated long enough to be lifted on to the Shetland Islands Council's ferry *Spes Clara* for transportation to Lerwick. Dennis then sought the advice of local boat builder Tommy Isbister, who told him that apart from the area under where the engine had been situated the rest of the wood was rotten down to the keel and the condition of the boat was worse than expected. Undaunted, Dennis employed Tommy to remove the previously heightened area and put in new boards to hold the boat together. In addition, Dennis arranged for Douglas Sinclair of Thulecraft to coat the *Advance* with black fibreglass, to resemble tar, and in 1980 the garage was built along with the roof we see today.[4]

It is not known when the original house on the promontory known as the Knoll or Knowe was built, but in 1798 a house "on the knowe of Loge Pund" is included in a list of properties owned by the late Arthur Nicolson.[5]

However, it is recorded in 1859 that the house and park was owned by Miss Grace Turnbull-Stewart (surviving daughter of the Rev. John Turnbull, Tingwall).[6] At that time the house was occupied by Thomas Anderson, a pilot. He had a son named Tammy, who also had a son named Tammy. The three were known as Aald Tammy, Young Tammy and Tammy o Middle Age. The middle age Tammy made fireworks, which he sold to young boys in the area.[7]

Captain Craigie's Well, said to be a large one situated at the foot of the knowe, was a deep well accessed by means of steps leading down to it.[8] However, during the building of his garage, Dennis found no trace of it.

By 1862 the area and house was the property of the Feuars and Heritors and the dwelling was occupied by John Arcus Brown, a blacksmith. John was born in 1830 at Rerwick, Bigton, to James Brown, blacksmith, and Barbara Arcus. In 1846 he came to Lerwick as an apprentice blacksmith to George Gillie, who had a 'smiddy' in a small courtyard near Stout's Court, opposite 10 Commercial Street. In 1857 John Brown married Margaret Gillie Brown, the granddaughter of George Gillie. When George died in 1861, John took over the business. However, he did not carry on at the old Gillie smiddy but instead moved to The Knowe. He was one of the best farriers in Shetland and considered to be the most skilful veterinary surgeon in the islands. In 1869 he bought Scottshall Court, opposite the Queens Hotel, but carried on his blacksmith business at The Knowe until he retired in 1888.[9]

In December of that year the old smiddy was entirely reconstructed and reverted back to a dwelling house with a new tenant, Andrew Irvine, joiner and contractor.[10]

Andrew and his wife, Christina Henderson, married in 1888 and had three children. Unfortunately, two of them died at a young age and when Christina died, in 1898, Andrew and his surviving son, Magnus Fredrick Francis Irvine, stayed on.[11] When Andrew died in 1928, occupancy of The Knowe passed to Fred, as he was better known.[12]

Fred, born in 1890, was a painter and decorator. A somewhat eccentric character, he fancied himself as an inventor, which can be surmised from an advertisement which appeared in *The Shetland Times* on 10th June 1911:

48. *Fred Irvine FRSA. c.1955*

"Irvines' Toothache Cure (Royal Patent). The only reliable cure on the market guaranteed to cure toothache in a few seconds. A child can use it. On sale by local chemists and druggists. Sole inventor and patenter Fred Irvine, The Knowe, Lerwick."

He obviously did not make his fortune from his invention because he carried on his trade from part of The Lodberrie, on Commercial Street, which he rented from 1917 until 1928 when the building caught fire[13] and was thereafter derelict for some time. In the 1930s, he opened the 'Bazaar' in Mounthooly Street (presently The Lounge Bar), where he sold everything from ironmongery, electrical goods and fancy goods to toys, gramophone records, confectionery, wallpaper, toilet goods and knitting wool. Prices were from 1d to 6d with nothing over 6d (2½p).[14]

Fred was an accomplished artist and illustrator and became a Fellow of the Royal Society of Arts, however, he is best remembered for his booklet *Shetland's Believe it or Not*, published in 1952. It contains a series, begun in *The Shetland News* in 1951, in which he illustrated 52 events and stories from Shetland's past and left readers to make up their own minds as to their authenticity. Due to the publication's popularity it was reprinted in 1955 and again in 1969, this time entitled *Pictures from Shetland's Past*. It would seem that the change in title upset local historian Mr E. S. Reid Tait to the extent that he found it necessary, in a newspaper letter, to point out factual errors in the publication.[15]

Fred was unperturbed by those allegations and was a 'weel kent' figure on Commercial Street, frequently seen deep in conversation with both locals and visitors alike, recalling events and tales of days gone by in Lerwick.[16] He died in the Brevik Hospital in 1976.

The Knowe was by now in poor condition and was vacant until purchased by Dennis and Muriel Coutts at a public auction in 1977. After major refurbishment, with the addition of an extension at the back with a grass roof, the Coutts family moved into their new home in 1980. Soon after, the rock face in front of the house was reinforced and the garage built. Evidence of the smiddy can be seen in a cupboard where the original hinges of the old smiddy door have been retained. In the 1990s a glass extension, 'the sea room', was added to the east side, which affords a stunning view of Lerwick harbour and Bressay Sound, allowing Dennis to pursue, in comfort, his lifelong passion for bird watching.[17]

Today The Knowe, complete with boat roof garage and the Shetland flag proudly flying, is one of the most photographed spots at the south end of Lerwick. Included in most images is the rock formation on the point below the house, called the 'Duke's Neb'. Often erroneously thought to be a deuk or duck's beak, it was so called because the outline was said to resemble the profile of the Duke of Wellington!

49. *Muriel & Dennis Coutts. 2017*

50. *"The Simmer Dim" from a painting by Fred Irvine.*

51. *An illustration by Fred in the author's autograph book depicting fictional smugglers.*

The Old Manse

52. *The Old Manse in 2007*

The Old Manse at 9 Commercial Street is believed to be the oldest inhabited house in Lerwick. A sasine indicates that William Dick, Scalloway, obtained a piece of land from Laurence Williamson on 12th September, 1683.[1] However, it is not known exactly when the house was built but the assumption is that it was soon after.

At that time there were no houses on the upper side of the street between the Old Manse and William Richan's house which was built in 1678. Richan's house was in the vicinity of the present-day Hayfield Court, earlier called Nice Court after Thomas Nice who was a tenant in the upper house in the court in the 1790s.[2]

The house commonly referred to as Patrick Torrie's, now 10 Commercial Street, was built on the lower side by Patrick Scollay about 1730.[3] It has been the home of Richard and Victoria Gibson since 1988.

The first Kirk in Lerwick was erected between 1660 and 1670 and part of it is incorporated into the present Masonic Hall.

In 1701 Lerwick was disjoined from Tingwall and became a separate parish. On 6th April, 1704, the Rev. James Milne was ordained as the first minister of the parish and the Heritors purchased the house[4] at 9 Commercial Street from William Dick[5] to serve as a manse for the new minister. The Rev. Thomas Waldie, the second minister from 1721-1739, bought the manse back from the Heritors[6] in 1722.

53. *A dwelling house and smithy on the left, then 7 Commercial Street, the Old Manse and 11 Commercial Street. In the centre is 10 Commercial Street and on the right is Copeland's House or 2-8 Commercial Street, and Gillie's Pier. 1880s*

Following the Rev. Waldie's death in 1739, his brother Walter sold the manse to James Craigie Snr. the same year.[7] The Rev. Waldie's widow Barbara who was related to James probably lived there until 1767. James Craigie Jnr., was living in the Old Manse in 1788[8] with his wife Margaret, née Ross. The Craigie family and descendants subsequently owned the Old Manse until 1907.

The last family member was Miss Grace Margaret Sands Turnbull-Stewart, who was James Craigie Snr's. great-granddaughter. When Grace inherited the property she was the only surviving child of the eight children of the Rev. John Turnbull, minister of Tingwall, and his wife Wilhelmina Sands. Mrs Turnbull, along with young daughter and son, Barbara and John, and also their maid, were tragically drowned in Tingwall Loch on 28th December, 1836.[9] [10] Grace Turnbull added Stewart to her name after inheriting property in 1853 from a relative in Orkney.[11]

Grace inherited a half share of the Old Manse in 1855, on the death of her mother's cousin, Capt. John Craigie of the 47th Regiment of Foot. He was a son of James and Margaret Craigie and had lived in the Old Manse since moving from Whiteness in 1840. Grace acquired the other half share of the property in 1858[12] from Elizabeth Grierson, née Craigie, who was her cousin and Capt. John Craigie's niece, but she let the house to John Mullay, who opened a lodging house there.[13] Grace lived in the Tingwall manse with her father until his death in 1867,[14] then moved into the Old Manse and remained there until her death in 1907.

It was the Craigie family who gave the name to the foreshore – Craigie Stane, situated to the south of The Lodberrie – as they also had property on what is now the site of Quendale House.

In 1907 following the death of the minister at Tingwall, the Rev. Alexander A. Bayne, his widow was the next owner of the Old Manse[15] and she resided there until her death in 1926.[16]

The house was subsequently bought by Mrs Margaret Fleurti from Kent who was

54. *A similar scene. Lower Leog is on the left, built about 1684 by William Craigie. The house and smithy are now roofless. The next building is 7 Commercial Street, then The Old Manse. 1950s*

a close relative of Mrs Bayne.[17] She did not live in the Old Manse but leased it to Laurence Arthur, an officer with HM Customs and Excise.[18] His son Stanley was later to become high commissioner in Barbados from 1978 until 1982 and was honoured for his work as a diplomat in the West Indies.[19]

In 1936 Mrs Fleurti sold the property to Gideon T. B. Robertson, merchant,[20] who later became a radio operator in the merchant navy. Unfortunately, he was tragically lost in 1941 through the sinking of his ship.[21] Subsequently, in 1942, his widow sold the Old Manse to Robert Jamieson, merchant, Sandness, and his son Andrew[22] who was county librarian. Andrew moved with his family to the Old Manse. Not long after his father's death he built a little cottage for his elderly mother on part of the grounds to the west, later occupied by Basil Wishart and family.[23] Andrew then left to work in the family business in Sandness and, incidentally, his son Bertie Jamieson expanded it and eventually built a spinning mill in the district.

The Old Manse was then acquired by William N. Sinclair[24] in 1947, who purchased it from Andrew Jamieson. Along with most old houses in Lerwick the east gable of the house faced the sea. At that time it had remained virtually unchanged over the years; a high wall surrounded the building on three sides, with access from Commercial Street by two wooden gates. One was to the south

55. *Capt. William and Mrs Marion Sinclair with family dog Vera in the Old Manse. Original wood panelling can be seen on the walls. Mid 1960s*

of the house, at the back, leading into a stone-flagged courtyard where at one time there was a well, said to contain excellent quality water, and a small wash house. The entrance was originally on this side of the house,[25] and the present front door would have been a first floor window.[26]

On the north side, a high wall with a wooden gate facing the sea opened on to a path leading to a porch, built in Victorian times, and inside were stone steps leading up to the front door, with wood cladding on the walls. On the left was the 'best room', or sitting room, which had original wooden wall panelling and shutters which were closed over the two windows that faced the sea during storms. The other window faced south.

On occasions the waves were so high that they occluded air from the chimney with the result that the fire was extinguished, forcing the family to move to the west end of the house. This was a spare sitting room containing a built-in bookcase and a piano. One potentially serious incident that occurred there provided an insight into the early construction of the house. The sudden appearance of a dark area on the wall above the fireplace suggested the presence of burning. An investigation revealed the source to be an ancient ship's beam which was smouldering. The kitchen and bathroom were between this room and the best room.

A staircase with cast-iron balusters and handrail led up to three bedrooms. The middle one, to the left of the staircase, had formerly been a child's room with a frieze depicting a nursery rhyme still adorning the walls. The other, in the east end, had two windows with shutters facing the sea, while the room at the west end had a large walk-in cupboard. A door to the right of the staircase was the entry, via wooden steps, to what the family called the 'fo'c's'le' (the forward part of a ship with the sailors' living quarters), but was actually a loft which was separated into two rooms used for storage.

In one room there was a small V-shaped oriel window at floor level facing the west, and it has been handed down that when the house was used as a manse a candle or lamp was lit in the window to guide the minister home. This, it could be argued, was highly unlikely as at that time the 'Auld Kirk' in Queens Lane was in use and an early map does not show any path leading from what is now South Hillhead towards Greenrig and to the manse.

Inside the front door a staircase led down to a cellar containing a small water closet, and two rooms which were occupied by a sitting tenant. A small porch led out to the courtyard situated at the south of the house and this was the original entrance. The kitchen would most probably have been located here.

Part of the garden at the west gable was sold to Lerwick Town Council to accommodate the Leog housing scheme built in 1958, and a children's play area.

The Sinclair family lived in the Old Manse until it was sold to Lerwick Town Council in 1965.[27] Partial refurbishment by Lerwick Town Council included a new WC and window at ground level and the installation of a kitchen in the spare sitting room. In 1967 the property was purchased by Alistair McDonald and his wife Laurna, who completed the restoration and added double windows to the kitchen and sitting room facing towards the north.[28]

The house was then bought in 1970 by Tom Henderson from Dunrossness. He represented Dunrossness North on Zetland County Council from 1952 for 11 years, and for the last three years he was also convener. He was appointed the first curator of the Shetland Museum in 1964, a post he held until his retiral in 1978. During this time a young student, none other than Mary Blance of BBC Radio Shetland fame, had a summer job at the museum and lodged at the Old Manse with Mr and Mrs Henderson. She could describe how the interior of the house had changed since the Sinclair family lived there. Following Mr Henderson's death in 1982 his widow stayed on in the house until her passing in 1989.

The Old Manse became a Grade B listed building in 1977.

Over the following years, the Old Manse changed hands several times, starting with Colin Forbes in 1990, then Irene and James Ross until 1994, followed by Marcia and Leslie Irving until 2000, during which time it was a guest house. It reverted back to a private house and the next owners were Carol and Patrick O'Connor until 2007, then Dorothy and James Cuthbert, until Danus Skene bought it in 2010. He remained there until his sudden death in August 2016[29].

56. *The Old Manse before the double windows on the front were added. c.1966*

Stout's Court

At Lerwick's historic south end there is an inconspicuous plaque on a wall at Stout's Court. It identifies the approximate site of the birthplace of Sir Robert Stout who, as a young man, emigrated to New Zealand and rose to prominence to become the prime minister of that country in 1884.[1]

In 1819 his grandfather, also named Robert, purchased "*a new house or warehouse, garden immediately above and adjoining kaleyard at head, also court in front and houses immediately downwards with yard/back close behind*" at the south end of Commercial Street from Charles Ogilvy, merchant and chief magistrate of Lerwick.[2] This property had previously belonged to various occupants of 10 Commercial Street, which is sometimes referred to as Patrick Torrie's house, on the opposite side of the street. Patrick lived there in the mid-1760s. The "new house" referred to above was built about 1754 and the "houses immediately downwards" is 17 Commercial Street, often referred to as 'Da Roost Hoose'.[3]

In the mid-1830s, Robert erected a new house: 15 Commercial Street with gable facing the street, also a pier opposite[4] still known as Stout's Pier, which is situated between 10 Commercial Street and Copeland's House (now 2-8 Commercial Street). He was a mason to trade and, among many other buildings, he was responsible for constructing Lerwick Parish Church (later St Columba's), along with son William and another mason from Aberdeen. They were responsible for hewing all the dressed stone.[5]

The gable of 17 Commercial Street also faced the street. Stout's Court was an open square at the upper end of the houses. Access could be gained from Commercial Street by a narrow passage between the houses at Nos. 15 and 17 and another between No.17 and Nice Court, which still exists, and at one time was called Ann Scollay's Closs.[6]

Robert was married to Grizal Williamson and they had two sons and two daughters. In 1838 a Disposition Deed of Settlement was registered, leaving houses in the Court to each of them. Robert died the following year. The elder son, Thomas Stout, inherited Robert's

57. Looking south towards 17 Commercial Street, Da Roost Hoose, which is extending into the street. On the left is 12 Commercial Street, on the right is Nice Court now Hayfield Court and in the centre is 2-8 Commercial Street, formerly Copeland's House. 1950s

58. *South Commercial Street looking towards the north with Mrs Cecilia Johnson's Cottage, then 15 Commercial Street with the shop sign, and No. 17 beyond. All were demolished in the 1960s. On the right is 10 Commercial Street which still exists*

recently built house at 15 Commercial Street. Thomas was a merchant and for many years he carried out business in a shop situated on the ground floor on the south court entrance. He also owned a house that stood on the site of the present Grand Hotel.[7] When he died, in 1879, the shop was taken over by his nephew James Sinclair, grocer. Later the premises was occupied by Margaret Jamieson, grocer and merchant, who, in 1918, married Edward Inkster, establishing the firm Inkster & Jamieson. In 1928 they opened a second shop at 59 Commercial Street, opposite the Queens Hotel, fondly remembered as 'Hairy Ned's'.[8]

The second son, William, was married to Barbara Nicol. He was left the original property acquired from Charles Ogilvy.

Robert's eldest daughter Barbara, married to James Sinclair, inherited the lower part of the property at 17 Commercial Street – a house of four rooms adjacent to Nice Court. Its gable jutted out into Commercial Street, leaving a very narrow thoroughfare known as The Roost, with his house being Da Roost Hoose.[9]

59. *Miss Margaret Jamieson outside her shop at 15 Commercial Street. c.1910*

James built Charlotte Place (the building now containing Harry's Department Store) for William Hay between 1827 and 1829, and the gas works (the site of Charlotte House, Commercial Road) in the 1850s. In 1847 he was responsible for the removal of five steps,[10] known as Miss Chalmers' Stairs, which crossed the street from the lower part of his property to 10 Commercial Street.[11] It was there that Miss Margaret Chalmers, the poetess, lived with her mother after they moved from Twageos House following the death of father, who was William Chalmers, collector of customs and factor for the Earl of Morton.[12] The removal of these steps opened up a cart passage to Leog and Twageos. Previous to this, cart access to Commercial Street was via Mounthooly Street as below Fort Charlotte was simply a narrow path, and Nort Kirk Closs (Queens Lane) was said at one time to have had steps.[13] In later years a small car could navigate through the space at the Roost with care.

Grizel, the younger sister, married John Brown, a blacksmith from Dunrossness, and they lived in 4 Stout's Court, the house at the upper end of and adjoining the Sinclair's house. John Brown's smithy was situated in a long narrow building adjoining the house to the north of Lower Leog. Their son, also named John, was a successful blacksmith and fish-curer who gave his name to Brown's Buildings at the north end of Burgh Road, and also Brown's Road.[14]

Both William and Thomas had sons called Robert who were to become well-known in their own right.

William's son Robert was born in Lerwick in 1841. He began his career as a shipping clerk, after which he was appointed to Lerwick Post Office. In 1863, at the age of only 22, he became post master, a position he held for 43 years.[15] On his retirement he entered public service, becoming a member of the town council, a bailie and then Provost of Lerwick from 1913 to 1915.[16]

Thomas's son Robert, already mentioned in the introduction to this article, was from the first marriage. He was born in what had been his grandparents' house at 15 Commercial Street. He became a pupil teacher at the parochial school at Clairmont Place (later the Baptist manse, now a private residence), where he was himself educated. He left Shetland at the age of 19 for New Zealand. He lived in Dunedin, where he taught at the grammar school. Having studied law he was admitted to the bar in 1871. In 1878 he became judge of the Lands Claim's Court and also an MP. He was elected to serve Dunedin in 1884 and was prime minister from 1884 to 1887. He then lost his seat but was re-elected. In 1886 he was created KCMG, and in 1899 was made chief justice, which post he held until he resigned in old age in 1926. He visited Shetland twice, in 1909 and 1927. Sir Robert died in 1930 at his home in Wellington.[17] Many Stout descendants live in New Zealand as well as in Shetland.

Over the years Stout's Court provided accommodation for numerous families at any given time. However, by the 1950s only da Roost Hoose was inhabited. To youths growing up in the vicinity the derelict buildings were an excellent playground and a safe refuge to enjoy the forbidden Woodbine.[18]

17 Commercial Street was obtained in 1938 by Zetland County Council. Lerwick Town Council obtained 15 Commercial Street in 1962.

Nothing remains of the original Stout's Court as all the buildings were demolished in the mid-1960s to be replaced by council-built flats and houses. However, the name was retained, thus creating a new Stout's Court.[19]

60. *This photograph taken in 1962 clearly shows the demise of Stout's Court, shown towards the bottom right. The ruin is Robert Stout's original property, later occupied by his son William. The dwelling and shop at 15 Commercial Street has been demolished. To the right of the courtyard is 17 Commercial Street, Da Roost Hoose. The next building is Nice Court, now Hayfield Court. Opposite Da Roost Hoose is 10 Commercial Street. The building to its left is 2-8 Commercial Street, formerly Copeland's House, which was renovated in 1967. The house opposite, 11 Commercial Street, was demolished along with the remaining Stout's buildings in the mid-1960s. The house to its left is the Old Manse, with Old Manse Cottage and Whitegates further up. Next to the Old Manse, and in front of Leog House (built 1868), is the Leog sheltered housing scheme. It was built in 1960 on the Leog House garden and on the site of Lower Leog House, two other houses and a smithy. On the left of the picture is Lovers Loan and the huts that were part of the HMS Fox naval base during the Second World War. In the bottom corner is The Knowe, originally a smiddy but occupied, at the time this photograph was taken, by the renowned local artist Fred Irvine, FRSA.*

By 1967, the Kveldsro Gardens housing scheme, built in the garden of Kveldsro House, and the Stout's Court scheme provided Lerwick with a further 21 local authority houses.

Kveldsro

Kveldsro Gardens is a housing scheme built in 1965 at Lerwick's historic south end, to a design by architect Richard Moira,[1] but the older generation will remember when the site was actually a large garden and lawn in the grounds of Kveldsro House. The owner, Arthur James Hay, was the youngest son of William Hay.

William Hay had bought a field from Arthur Nicolson of Lochend in 1825 on which he built his mansion, Hayfield House, which was completed by 1830.[2] At that time William was a partner in the firm Hay & Ogilvys but, following the collapse of the company in 1842, he joined two of his sons, William and Charles, in 1844 as Hay & Company.[3] They soon left Shetland leaving their father and brother George to run the business.[4] Following William's death in 1858, George took his young brother Arthur James into the firm.[5] The firm exists today as Hay & Company Buildbase.

Arthur built his house on part of the extensive Hayfield Estate in 1870 and named it Kveldsro House,[6] commonly pronounced Kelro. In Norwegian it means 'evening rest' or 'peace'.

61. *Mr Arthur James Hay. c.1870s*

62. *Kveldsro House from the air. Kveldsro Cottage is behind and Kveldsro Gardens housing scheme is in front with Nice Court, now Hayfield Court, below. c.1966*

63. *On the lawn at Kveldsro are from left: Miss Helen Christie, Miss Urcilla Robertson and Mrs Ruby Murray. The Widows' Homes, now Anderson Homes, are in the background and Midgarth House is on the right. c.1930*

64. *The back garden, vegetable plot and greenhouse at Kveldsro House. c.1904*

65. *The Robertson family in front of Kveldsro Cottage. c.1900*

The extensive lawn was at the front of the house facing towards the east, and from there a panoramic view of Bressay Sound could be enjoyed. A path led down to Nice Court (now Hayfield Court), which was also part of the Hayfield Estate.

A greenhouse was attached to the back of the house with a vegetable plot and rose garden beyond. Roses were taken on Fridays during the summer to Hayfield House to grace the tables at weekend dinner parties.[7]

To the west of the vegetable plot was the stable, and Kveldsro Cottage where the Robertson family lived. Gilbert was the gardener/handyman/groom, and his wife Elizabeth was the family's cook and head servant.[8] Their daughter Urcilla was a personal companion to Miss Margaret Elizabeth Hay, the only child of Arthur and his wife Charlotte.

On the death of his brother George in 1890, Arthur Hay became the principal partner and head of the firm Hay & Company, the largest employer of labour in Shetland at that time.[9] His daughter succeeded to the Hayfield Estate on his death in 1896.[10]

Miss Hay, educated in England and Germany, lived in either Kveldsro House or Hayfield House during the summer and spent the winter months south. In addition to taking an active interest in Hay & Company she was an excellent singer and talented musician who also played the organ in the Adam Clarke Memorial Methodist Church. She was a generous benefactor to many causes and a member of The Dorcas Society and Lerwick Nursing Association.

66. Gilbert Robertson in front of Kveldsro House

Miss Hay died in 1937[11] and Colonel Westwood Norman Hay, a grandnephew of Arthur Hay, inherited the Hayfield Estate in 1939.[12] During the Second World War both Hayfield House and Kveldsro House were taken over by the Shetland Defence Battalion. Tents were erected between Kveldsro House and Cottage to act as a mess for the troops billeted at the Glebe, otherwise known as Mansefield (the field between Clumlie, the former Church of Scotland manse, and the section of Breiwick Road adjacent to the Old Cemetery).[13]

For a short time members of the Shetland Defence Company, commonly referred to as 'Da Blinnd Hunder', occupied Kveldsro Cottage. The name was coined by local fishcurer Joe Mair to contrast Da Blinnd Hunder with Lord

67. Miss Margaret Elizabeth Hay in the greenhouse at Kveldsro House. c.1900

Tennyson's 'Six Hundred' immortalised in his poem *The Charge of the Light Brigade*. Later, Christie Tulloch from Northmavine composed a poem with a tune added by Tom Anderson.[14]

Two Lewis guns were installed on the lawn in front of Kveldsro House, which on one occasion saw action when attempting to shoot down a Dornier aircraft which was attacking the cable ship *Ariel* lying in the harbour.[15]

The house remained in the family until 1949 when Colonel Hay's son, Captain John (Jock) Westwood Hay, sold it to the Herring Industry Board for staff accommodation.[16] It then became the residence of Mr Alex Duthie, HIB manager, his wife Eliza and daughter Elizabeth,[17] also Mr Thomas Bolt, engineer, and his wife Grace.[18] In 1946 the Herring Industry Board had built a factory on the site of the Anglo-Scottish herring station,[19] previously John Brown's Station. Mareel now covers part of the site.

Lerwick Town Council bought part of the Kveldsro grounds from the HIB in 1956 and the housing scheme, accurately named Kveldsro Gardens, was built in 1965.

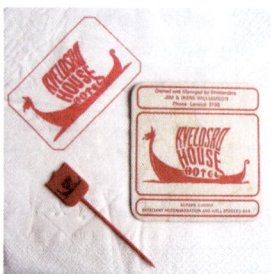

68. *Jim & Irene's Kveldsro House Hotel logo shown on serviette, beer mat and cocktail stick*

69. *Irene and Jim Williamson with staff in 1975. From left: Linda Williamson, Irene, Charlie Holland, Jasmine Tulloch, Leslie Setrice, Anna Smith, Bob Conroy, Alison McHattie, Jim, Rita Simpson. Front: George Sandison and Rosemary Shaw*

The remaining garden and house was bought by the town council in 1966[20] and was converted to provide eight hostel bedrooms on the first floor with a three-apartment flat, dining room and kitchen on the ground floor. The intention was to provide accommodation for female workers but it was fully occupied only for a brief period when used by both males and females. The whole venture was unsuccessful and the decision was made in November 1967 to dispose of the property.[21]

However, as prominent as the Hay family was in Lerwick for well over 170 years, when mentioning Kveldsro nowadays the name that springs to mind is not Hay but Williamson. Namely Jim Williamson, otherwise known as 'Hoover Jim' and his wife Irene. He received the nickname through an earlier very successful career as salesman for Hoover products in Shetland. The couple acquired the property in November 1968 and the following April, after extensive refurbishment, Kveldsro House Hotel was born.[22] With Jim's friendly jovial manner it soon become one of the most popular pubs in Lerwick and 'regulars' soon gathered there after work on Fridays. The Williamsons were staunch supporters of the RNLI of which Jim at one time was president of the local branch. His support and admiration for the Institution was reflected in the photographs of Lerwick waterfront by Dennis Coutts which adorned the walls of the hotel.

The car park was created early in 1973 and the bar was extended the following year. At the same time an extension at the back provided a large kitchen and eight additional bedrooms.

With assistance from Jasmine Tulloch, who was promoted to manageress in 1981, the clientele rose from strength to strength. Evening meals were served in the elegantly decorated dining room. Bar lunches were introduced later and this initiative came about following a cancelled booking. Rather than waste the food, Irene offered beefsteak pie with chips to three senior school pupils who happened to be there that lunchtime. From their feedback it was decided to give bar lunches a try and this proved to be so successful that very often 120 lunches were prepared per day. Bar suppers were introduced soon after. Occasionally there were music nights.[23]

Unfortunately, this all sadly came to an end when Jim passed away very suddenly on 16th June, 1991.[24] Many people have very fond memories of Jim and evenings spent at Kveldsro.

That same year the hotel was taken over and later traded along with the Grand and Queens hotels as KGQ Hotels. Following refurbishment it could be argued that Kveldsro lost much of its previous charm.

In February 2004, Kveldsro House Hotel was sold to the Brudolff Hotels Group, which includes The Lerwick Hotel, The Shetland Hotel and the Craighaar Hotel in Aberdeen.[25]

70. *Jim & Irene Williamson, behind the bar in Kveldsro House Hotel, celebrating 20 years in business. 1988*

71. *The South End from the air. The Stout's Court housing scheme is under construction and behind the upper row is the Kveldsro lawn and house. c.1966*

CRAIGIE'S COURT AND QUENDALE HOUSE

On the site of Quendale House stood the town house of Bailie James Craigie. The house was described as consisting of a square, or courtyard, on the front entered by an arched-way and on the top, carved into the stone, was the date 1737. (This stone also included the Craigie family coat of arms bearing the initials JC and EH – James Craigie and his wife Elizabeth Henderson.) The southern side of the square, which formed a complete enclosure, was flanked by a very old house of six rooms tenanted by six different families. Opposite the archway was the garden gate and short walls extended from there on either side. The northern side of the square was composed of a one-storey house of four or six rooms with gable facing the street, also another small tenement occupied by the town scavengers, Margaret Edinburgh and Margaret Green. This court used to be called Craigie's Court.[1] Although these two women may have been so in their younger days, both are listed in the 1851 census for Lerwick – the former as a stocking knitter in Craigie's Court and the latter as a pauper, formerly a hosiery knitter, living in Navy Lane.

From the street the house looked like an inverted L, the end of the long stalk resting on the edge of the street and the foot of the letter pointing northwards, and forming the back of the courtyard. Tacked on to the south of the gable facing the shore was a tiny shed-like structure, with one small window overlooking the street. Along the front, approximately in the line of the railings of the modern Quendale House, was the courtyard wall, the gate being towards the northern end. The grounds of the house were approximately the same as those of the present Quendale House.[2]

James Craigie is thought to have died in 1741. His grand-nephew, also called James Craigie, ultimately inherited the property and he passed it on to his son, Capt. John Craigie, who lived in the Old Manse. By this time the property was referred to as Miss Craigie's House and she is believed to have been Bailie Craigie's daughter Catherine.

72. *Quendale House is in the centre with the Craigie Stane and The Lodberrie in front. c.1966*

Following John's death in 1855, it ultimately passed to his niece Elizabeth Craigie.[3] She was married to James Grierson. In 1864-65 their son, Andrew John Grierson of Quendale and his wife Alice Geraldine Clifford, built a new town house on the site.[4] His previous house, also called Quendale House (now The Stage Door) was next to Quendale Lane, previously known as Grierson's Closs. One of their sons, Sir Herbert J. C. Grierson, was born in the new house and had a distinguished career. He was the first professor of literature at Aberdeen University and was an authority on the subject.[5] Andrew died in 1896 and it would appear his widow and members of the family stayed on in the house for some time.[6]

In 1906-07, Mr J. C. C. Broun, who had recently been appointed sheriff-substitute at Lerwick, became a tenant of Quendale House and remained there until the outbreak of the First World War when he moved south.[7]

The next tenant (1914-15) was Robert Anderson, draper, of the Lerwick firm of Anderson & Co at 60-62 Commercial Street. He bought the house in January 1918.[8] His brother Thomas, a partner in Anderson & Co, and John Bannatyne, a Lerwick solicitor and founder of the present firm of solicitors J. B. Anderson & Goodlad, lived in Quendale House along with Robert. Both Robert and Thomas predeceased John Bannatyne who became owner of the house until his death in 1937.

The next owner was Mr Ovington, a dentist, with his wife and young family.[9] During the Second World War, Quendale House was taken over by the Admiralty and a good number of Wrens (Women' Royal Naval Service) were based there and at HMS Fox naval base at Midgarth.[10] Mr and Mrs Ovington and their children moved to Prospect House, Law Lane, but they eventually sold Quendale House to the postmaster-general in 1946.[11] Thereafter for some time it was the residence of the head postmaster of Shetland.

In 1883 Shetland's first telephone connected Hay & Company's offices, in the former lodberry at the north of the Queens Hotel, with Hayfield House. A small public switchboard was installed in the Post Office in the Old Tolbooth in the early 1900s, but Shetland's first telephone exchange switchboard was installed, on 26th August 1907, in a room rented from a Gilbertson family in their house at 12 St Magnus Street, Lerwick. As the demand continued to grow, a larger unit was installed in June 1925 to provide a 24-hour telephone service within Shetland. There it remained until a decision was made to relocate to Quendale House and installation work began in 1949. The telephone exchange came into action on the 10th May, 1950.[12]

The postmaster had to move to the top storey which was accessible by an external metal stair at the back of the house. This probably explains the addition of dormer windows, for earlier photographs show the house without these.[13]

Quendale House continued as the telephone exchange until 26th March, 1975, when the Shetland telephone system was switched over from manual to the new automatic exchange nearby, connecting Lerwick with the national STD (subscriber trunk dialling) network. The switchboard, which had been installed in 1950, was the last of its type working in the UK and was now redundant. Provost J. J. Taylor inaugurated the switchover.[14] A reduced number of switchboard operators moved to the new building, but in 1987 the telephone exchange closed when operator services were transferred to Aberdeen.

73. *Lerwick Telephone Exchange switchboard in Quendale House*

A postmaster and an engineer lived on in Quendale House for some time, after which it stood vacant.

Quendale House became a Category B listed building on 18th October, 1977.[15]

Shetland Leasing and Property (SLAP) purchased Quendale House in May 1982 and provided a long-term lease to Shetland Islands Council. The administration department moved from the County Buildings and remained there until 1997. Adult services (part of community care), was the next council occupant.

Shetland Islands Council acquired the property from SLAP in 2008 and it continued to be used as council offices. In 2012 the supported living and outreach management and senior team moved from Quendale House to the Grantfield community health and social care offices.

74. *George Barrie and Beth Peterson at work. c.1970*

Quendale House was then closed and the following year Shetland Islands Council corporate services invited offers for lease of the building. In 2015 the property was leased to Shetland FM, the present tenants.[16]

Today there are two reminders of the Craigie family. During the demolition of Craigie's Court in the early 1860s, the stone bearing the family coat of arms was saved. When the construction of the Town Hall began in 1881, Arthur Laurenson, a local merchant, requested its builder John M. Aitken to incorporate the stone in the north gable of the building.[17] This was duly carried out, however, it was said that Mr Aitken did not appreciate being told what to do. He consequently placed

the stone high on the gable above the Rose Window, under the peak,[18] and it remained there until 1996 when, following a request from Shetland Museum staff, it was removed to prevent further erosion. It was placed for safety in the nearby Shetland Museum and is now stored at the present museum.

When walking south along Commercial Street the large, slanting, solid rock, appropriately called the Craigie Stane,[19] can be seen at the shore below the wall opposite Quendale House. During a violent storm in 1900, the sea broke over Commercial Street and the lower parapet wall at the Craigie Stane was destroyed. It was believed to have been one of Lerwick's oldest landmarks.[20]

75. The Craigie Coat of Arms

76. The Craigie Stane with part of Bain's Court upper left and The Lodberrie to the right. 1920s

THE LODBERRIE

77. The Lodberrie with the Craigie Stane in the foreground. 2006

Lodberries were an integral part of Old Lerwick's waterfront. The word lodberry derives from Old Norse *hladberg*, a landing rock,[1] but in the Lerwick context it applies to a stone store built out into the sea, at which goods could be directly transferred to or from vessels and boats.[2] The merchants, whose houses were nearby, had them built as a convenient means of unloading supplies and goods which had been transported by sea in the days before piers were built. Lodberries had another purpose too – namely to facilitate the covert practice of smuggling Dutch gin, tobacco and tea. The merchants who lived on the landward side of the street had tunnels built from their lodberries to exit either in their house or a skilfully concealed outlet in a convenient garden.[3]

The first lodberry was built about 1730 by Patrick Scollay at the back of his house, now 10 Commercial Street,[4] often referred to as Patrick Torrie's house after a later occupant. By 1814 there were 21 lodberries.[5] In 1817, when Orcadian James Copland built his lodberry[6] at the rear of a row of houses between Stout's Pier and Gillie's Pier (2-8 Commercial Street), they stretched along the waterfront from near Leog beach to the North Lodberry, which is where Harry's Department Store and Westside Pine is now situated.

With the construction of the Esplanade in the early 1880s most of the lodberries disappeared, but some were converted: Tait's Lodberry became the Thule Bar; Grieg's Lodberry is the Peerie Shop and Cafè; while Leask's Lodberry is to be found to the north of the rear of the Post Office, behind Anderson & Goodlad Solicitors.

At the south end, the old Steamers' Store Lodberry, situated to the south of the Craigie Stane, has changed little, while the dwelling to its north – simply called The Lodberrie – is the subject of this article.

The walls of The Lodberrie are virtually unchanged since its construction about 1772 by a merchant named James Linklater, who had property on the opposite side of the street.[7] Still surrounded by the sea on three sides, The Lodberrie stands between Bain's Beach and the Craigie Stane. In 1823 the trustees of James's late son George, who was married to Jane Sands, sold The Lodberrie to her brother-in-law, the Rev. John Turnbull,[8] who was the minister of the parish church of Tingwall. He used as his town house the property opposite, previously owned by the Linklaters and later known as Irvinesgord.

In 1859 the Rev. Turnbull sold The Lodberrie to Bailie John Robertson.[9] It is thought to have consisted of steps leading down to noosts at the Craigie Stane with an entrance leading to a kitchen and office, a store for boats and gear, a wet fish store, and also an area for storing masts and spars. North, east and south-facing sea doors allowed the transfer of cargo to and from boats at all times, depending on the tides. At Commercial Street level there was a shop above a cellar, parlour, bedroom, a sail loft with dry goods store and a skeo for drying fish and meat.[10]

At the Craigie Stane there was an old sea defence wall that was swept away with the force of the sea during the great storm of 16th February, 1900.[11]

78. *As seen from the sea. The former Steamers' Store Lodberry is on the left and, prior to the opening of Victoria Pier in 1886, the steamers anchored in the harbour and goods were transported here by flit boat. The Lodberrie is to the right.*

79. *The Lodberrie and derelict shop before restoration. 1950s*

Robertson's Lodberry, as it was commonly known, was used for various functions including the slaughtering of farm animals[12] – as were most lodberries. Dutch fishermen came ashore here to obtain drinking water from the draw-well at the narrow closs at the north side of Water Lane. They then rolled their water barrels down past Craigie Stane into the lodberry from where they loaded them directly on to their vessels.[13]

John Robertson sold the property in 1885 to John Harrison with assignation by him to the firm of J. T. Garriock & Company. The North of Scotland Bank Ltd was the next owner from 1887 until 1900 when it was sold to John Irvine, commission agent, son of William Irvine. On John's death it passed to his nephew, William Irvine Hunter, and then to Miss Beatrice Hunter in 1933.[14] She lived nearby in Irvinesgord – the house previously owned by her grandfather William Irvine and earlier by Miss Grace M. Turnbull-Stewart, who lived in the Old Manse.

Fred Irvine, the well-known local artist and house painter who lived at The Knowe, rented the shop from 1917 until 1928 when, following a fire, it became derelict.[15] However, the dwelling house part of the The Lodberrie was unaffected and was home to the Paton and Johnson families until the mid-1930s, when they moved to new houses.[16] It then became vacant. A south end resident can remember as a boy in the late 1930s seeing barrel hoops being made at Craigie Stane and the interior of The Lodberrie stacked high with barrels, which were subsequently transported by flit boats.[17]

The property lay in a derelict condition until 1956 when Mr Thomas Moncrieff, commonly known as Tammy, leased the premises. He subsequently bought the property from Miss Hunter in 1961 and began a surreptitious restoration programme because he knew that if he applied for planning permission it would be refused.[18] He succeeded in reinstating the building and resided there with his wife Muriel until his death in 2005. It is now the home of his son Erik.

Over the years The Lodberrie has become a well-photographed landmark and a testament to Tammy's vision and tenacity in undertaking the restoration of the old building at a time when many of the south end's historic houses were demolished to make way for modern flats. His efforts were worthwhile as it is now a Class A listed building.

At the present time it is a popular tourist attraction following the screening of the *Shetland* crime series on television. The Lodberrie is portrayed as the home of Jimmy Perez, the main character.

80. *Tammy Moncrieff*

BAIN'S COURT, RAVEN'S COURT, WATER LANE AND IRVINESGORD

81. *Bain's Court, Raven's Court, Water Lane and Lochend House. 1932*

For clarity it may be simpler to identify the buildings at Bain's Court, Raven's Court and Water Lane shown on this photograph rather than provide a detailed history as the various properties changed hands many times.

The building on the left was Fred Irvine's shop in the 1920's and is now part of The Lodberrie. Directly opposite were houses at Bain's Court. Next to the doorway with the steps leading to what was at one time the Customs House, was an arch or trance[1] with a small courtyard beyond with steps leading to a dwelling directly ahead.

The row of houses at Raven's Court were adjacent on the right. Above the entrance to the trance were the words "*Pro deo, pro rege, et patria*" translated as "*For God, for king, and country*".[2] A joist was a helm taken from an old Dutch fishing vessel[3] and when the building was demolished it was removed to the Shetland Museum.

Bain's Court with Bain's Beach opposite were named after James Bain, a joiner and auctioneer who lived with his large family in Lochend House, which he had purchased from Arthur Nicolson of Lochend in 1818. In the 1840s, the Bain family had a tame eagle as a pet who perched on top of the courtyard's gateway to keep a lookout for children. They were afraid of it due to the fact that it pecked the food out of their hands as they passed by.[4]

Gilbert, one of James's sons, was a merchant and spent some time in Singapore. Following his death at Edinburgh in 1886, his sisters bequeathed money for the erection of a hospital to be named in memory of their brother. It was built at the corner of Scalloway Road with King Harald Street and opened in 1902.[5] The former hospital is now Goudie's Funeral Directors Ltd. When the present hospital was built at the foot of Gilbertson Road in 1961, the name was retained.

Before the Bain family owned property in Bain's Court it was earlier called Sands' Court, most likely due to the fact that the Rev. James Sands, who was the fourth minister of Lerwick from 1767 until 1793, and family members had property in the court.[6]

82. *A portrait of Gilbert Bain*

In the photograph on the previous page a man can be seen walking in front of the entrance to Raven's Court where the lower house in the row of houses is visible.

The house at Water Lane was originally the town house of the Dicks of Fracafield and was built prior to 1774. The narrow 'trinkie' between Water Lane and Lochend House was Draw-well Closs. So called from the well which was at the top of the closs.[7]

The entrance to the courtyard of Lochend House is shown on the right. The house was built, or rebuilt, about 1760 and was originally the town house of Arthur Nicolson of Lochend.

83. *The upper part of Raven's Court with the west gable of Irvinesgord on the right. c.1880s*

84. Print from lithograph entitled 'Lerwick', with shipping in the foreground in the mid-1800s, by John Irvine, RSA

To return to the passage at the entrance to Raven's Court, it led to the courtyard at the back of Bain's Court and towards a large house which faced east[8]. It has been written that Raven's Court was so called due to the Misses Campbell's pet raven.[9] In the early 1800s, the Campbell family lived in that house and sisters Dorothea Primrose and Eliza Matilda Campbell ran a private school in Lerwick for the education of daughters of the local gentry.[10]

Of all the houses in the courts, the house that was later to be named Irvinesgord is probably the one that is best known. It was joined to the previously mentioned house, facing in the direction of what is now Quendale House, and had many owners and residents. Prior to 1716 it was occupied by Magnus Gray and his wife. That year Alexander Davidson was the proprietor and he was followed by his son John, who died, aged 33, in 1751, following a drowning accident. His gravestone was the large memorial that could be seen in the Auld Kirkyard, now Church Road car park.

85. Miss Beatrice Hunter in her garden at Irvinesgord. c.1960

The house was sold to James Linklater in 1782[11] and ultimately passed on through his daughter-in-law Jane Sands to her sister Barbara[12] and then to her niece, Grace M. Turnbull-Stewart.[13] Her father, the Rev. John Turnbull, used the property as his town house but there is no evidence that he owned it. Furthermore, it is erroneously claimed that Sir Walter Scott dined with the Rev. Turnbull at this house when he visited Shetland in 1814, but the event actually took place at the Tingwall manse, his main residence.[14]

Grace sold the house in 1866 to William Irvine[15], merchant, and it became the Irvine family home later to be named Irvinesgord. His son was the renowned portrait artist

John Irvine, RSA, who emigrated to New Zealand and died there in 1888. Thirty of his works that were displayed at Irvinesgord are now housed in Shetland Museum and Archives.[16] Miss Beatrice Hunter, who was John Irvine's grand-niece, inherited the house. She was a pleasant interesting person and a brilliant linguist who had spent many years in Sweden. In addition she was an accomplished musician who had played first violin in the Lerwick Orchestra. Always willing to share her knowledge and memories with visitors who were ensured a warm welcome in her home.[17] She died in 1967 and was the last occupant of Irvinesgord.

Bain's Court, lower Raven's Court and Water Lane were all demolished in the early 1960s to be replaced in 1965 by two blocks of flats called, appropriately, Water Lane.

Irvinesgord and the adjoining house in Raven's Court were demolished later to provide a site for the new automatic telephone exchange.

86. *Flats at Water Lane. 2017*

'STEBBAGRIND'S HOUSE' OR SEAFIELD COURT

Before the various buildings comprising the Queens Hotel came into existence the property of Robert Craigie, commonly known as 'Stebbagrind's House', would have enjoyed an open view of Bressay Sound.[1] It was passed to his son James in 1778, apparently in a ruinous condition, and then sold to Francis Yates in 1787. His lodberry opposite ultimately became incorporated into the Queens Hotel. Yates's son, also Francis, inherited the property in 1824.

Charles Ogilvy became the next owner of the whole tenement of houses known as Stebbagrind's House in 1835.[2] He changed the name to Seafield Court after the family property at Seafield, Sound, and it became his town house.[3] The address is 49 Commercial Street.

After the collapse of the firm Hay & Ogilvy in 1842, Seafield Court was purchased by John Stout of Graven in 1845 from the sequestrated estate of Charles Ogilvy.[4] The property remained in the Stout family until bought by Joseph Leask. It then passed to his heirs in 1866 and stayed in the Leask family until 1935, when it was purchased by Bruce Sinclair.[5] Ownership remains in the family.

The shop at street level has had several occupants over the years.

One that holds special memories for many people is Irvine's Hairdressing Salon where, in 1932, the staff pioneered the field of permanent waving by introducing Eugene Waving. Many years later the firm still considered this process *"to be the premier method of safe, harmless, comfortable and satisfactory waving of hair"* according to an advertisement. Full head perms ranged from the equivalent of £1.10 to £2.50 in the early 1950s.[6]

The owner was George Irvine, commonly known as Dovis, who along with his son Joe and daughter Hilda ran the popular hairdressing business, assisted by Bella Scott, née Sinclair, who actually lived in the building. Although mainly catering for women, male customers could occasionally receive a trim. In the late 1940s and early 1950s an additional service was introduced when, by means of a converted bus, a full hairdressing service was provided to country areas. Later on, Hilda often travelled to Unst on the North Isles vessel *Earl of Zetland* where she extended the service to local people at the Springfield Hotel.[7]

Later occupiers of the shop were Maka Knitwear of Shetland, L. & M. Anderson, Intrigue, The Wendy House, Shetland Craft, The Magpie's Nest and Shetland Antiques & Collectables to name but a few.

87. *Over the years the buildings shown in this photograph, taken in the late 1990s, remained almost unaltered with only the various shops changing hands. Elizabeth Johnston's Spider's Web shop is in Lochend House on the left, but in the 1970s it was knitwear shop too, called Jean the Shetland Knitter, operated by Jean McPherson, née Jarmson, who also lived in the house.*

The small white building was for many years Mimie Peterson's knitwear shop while next door is Seawinds, occupied at this time by the Citizens Advice Bureau (CAB) but previously it was Jack Peterson's butcher shop. He was Mimie's husband and commonly known as Patter, as was their son Bobby. Seafield Court, previously Irvine's Hairdressing Salon, is by now the Shetland Craft shop. The next building is Scottshall Court and opposite is the Queens Hotel. Bain's Beach is in the foreground.

The Queens Hotel

88. Bain's Beach with the Queens Hotel to its right

Standing proudly in the sea at Lerwick's historic south end, the Queens Hotel dominates the waterfront and has done so since 1868, but the buildings which comprise the hotel were previously a combination of – at various times – houses, offices, shops, and lodberries.

The story begins in 1804 when James Hay, along with his sons, took the first step towards establishing a retail trade. They acquired a site to the east of the Old Tolbooth and built a small house with a stone jetty and warehouse where goods could be transported ashore from vessels anchored in the harbour.[1] This became known as Hay's Lodberry and an open space between it and Murray's workshop or lodberry was known as Murray's Hol, as in olden days under the cover of darkness contraband was said to have been smuggled ashore. It is believed that there was a tunnel from there to houses at Scottshall Court on the opposite side of Commercial Street, where John Murray lived in the late 1700s.[2]

At a roup in 1807, William, one of James's sons, bought a new house, offices, a shop, cellars and lodberry that had been built by Nicol Sinclair,[3] next to the property built in 1804. The house became the Hay family residence.[4]

William went into partnership with his father-in-law Charles Ogilvy in 1822, creating the firm Hay & Ogilvys who were import and export agents. That same year the firm

89. Hay's Steps were adjacent to Hay's Lodberry which was built in 1804. Early 1880s

90. George H. B. Hay who created the Queens Hotel

established the Shetland Bank which issued its own banknotes until 1828. William carried on his own retail business but, in 1825, this was merged with the firm and after 1832 the business became Hay & Ogilvy. Unfortunately the firm and bank were declared bankrupt in 1842 and properties were put in the hands of trustees.

In 1844, following the collapse of the company, William Snr joined his sons William and Charles in business under Hay & Company[5]. Both sons went south that same year leaving their father and their brother, George Husband Baird Hay, to carry on the business.[6] In 1857 George acquired the properties from his father including the shop, cellar, lodberry and new house.[7]

After William Snr died in 1858, George inherited the Hayfield Estate. He carried on trading and took his young brother Arthur James into partnership,[8] and records would suggest that the headquarters and shop were in the premises built in 1804. The firm exists today as Hay & Company Buildbase at Freefield.

In 1836 William Hay had bought Francis Yates's lodberry which was to the south of his property[9] and, in 1845, it was bought from William's estate by John Henry, a boot and shoemaker.[10] He built a house and shop over the lodberry with an entrance from a balcony overlooking Bain's Beach.[11] In the early 1850s, John emigrated to Australia, where he died in 1856, and his wife followed with some of her family in 1857.[12] Robert Henry, John's son and heir, sold the property to George H. B. Hay in 1866.[13]

George moved his family into Hayfield House, which his father had built in 1830, and in 1868 he converted his former residence, the houses on each side, a lodberry and shop, to create the Queens Hotel. He then leased it out.

Hay & Company continued to occupy the north part of the premises as their offices and have the distinction of installing the first private telephone in Shetland, in 1883, linking the offices with Hayfield House.[14]

The first proprietor of the Queens Hotel was a Caithness man, Thomas Evans, who along with his wife was reported as being experienced in the business. He had a stock of horses and conveyances for hire.[15] The Queens was said to be a 20-30 bedded "*first-class hotel, the finest premises in Lerwick*". His business was short lived, however, as by 1870 it was in sequestration[16] and he moved to Orkney.[17]

In 1872, the next leaseholder was James Connon, who was also proprietor of the Kirkwall Hotel. He advertised the premises as "*the only licensed hotel in Shetland, complete with thirty bedrooms, a number of Private Parlours, a large Coffee Room and a magnificent Commercial Room*". Excellent trout fishing in a number of lochs through Shetland was promoted.[18]

The hotel prospered and was a popular venue for both businessmen and tourists. An advertisement in 1881,[19] by the proprietor Alexander Henderson, stated that a boat from the Queens met the steamers on arrival and from their anchorage conveyed passengers, plus luggage, direct to the hotel. (At that time the Victoria Pier had not yet been built.)

91. *The Old Tolbooth on the left, Mr Levack's saddle shop on the right, with model of white horse in the window, and part of the Queens Hotel in the background. Late 1870s*

However, in 1887 the Queens was the venue for a banquet following the opening of Victoria Pier. George Sinclair, proprietor, submitted an account for £44 for wine, but Lerwick Harbour trustees argued that as some of the wine had been returned unopened they were only willing to pay £31![20]

George H. B. Hay died in 1890 and his brother Arthur inherited the Hayfield estate.

92. *The Queens Hotel on the right showing the original entrance. c.1885*

93. The south part of the hotel before the additional rooms were added in 1910. It was formerly Yates's Lodberry and then the Henry family residence

As the head of Hay & Co he was the largest employer of labour in Shetland. Following his death in 1896 the Hayfield estate passed to his only child, Miss Margaret Elizabeth Hay.[21]

The Queens Hotel continued to thrive and as a consequence an additional ten rooms were built on the south side of the establishment in 1910, extending what had earlier been the Henry family home.[22]

In 1914 Lerwick Harbour Trust constructed the breakwater and created the small boat harbour. This move was detrimental to the hotel as the backwash from the pier began to cause damage to the lodberry foundation. A legal dispute lasting from 1915 to 1917 between Miss Hay and Lerwick Harbour Trust was resolved by the building of a protective sea wall.[23]

What could potentially have been a serious incident occurred in 1926. Electricity was not available in Lerwick until the early 1930s and until then the town was lit by gas. Early one morning towards the end of November a maid lit a gas burner in the chandelier suspended from the roof in the Commercial Room within the hotel. Soon after, there was an explosion followed by the sound of breaking glass. The room was extensively damaged with a large hole blown in the brick partition and three windows facing Commercial Street also blown out. Remarkably, a large mirror and items of furniture were undamaged and there were no reports of injuries. In addition, the large plate glass window was damaged in Mr Harris's ladies' outfitter shop on the opposite side of the street[24] (until 2016 the Lodberrie Deli, then From Shetland with Love).

After the death of Miss Hay in 1937 ownership of the Queens Hotel buildings remained in the family when her cousin, Colonel Westwood Norman Hay, inherited the estate in 1939.

The hotel continued to be run by a series of managers. One was Donald Swanson, originally from Thurso, who at the outbreak of the First World War was employed in the hotel. He immediately joined the Royal Navy and was subsequently posted for

94. *A glass porch replaced the original entrance. 1950s*

duty in Shetland waters. In 1929 he took over the Queens from the proprietor George Sherman, who moved to Biggar. Over the years, Donald built up the business and introduced many modern improvements, such as hot and cold water in every bedroom and, in 1939, he purchased the hotel from the Hay family.[25] His son Stanley was actually born in the Queens Hotel and he also became a well-known and successful local businessman.

The function room was used as an Up-Helly-A' hall from before the First World War until 1975, but was not popular with guizers due to the restricted space in the narrow corridors.

In 1948 the hotel was sold to Yell man, Laurence T. Thomason,[26] merchant, who incidentally was Guizer Jarl in 1954. Two years later, in 1956, local businessman Alexander I. Tulloch bought the hotel and traded as Queens Hotel of Shetland Limited.[27] He also owned the Shetland hosiery business Tulloch of Shetland.

A popular holiday job for schoolboys in the early1960s was as a hotel 'boots',[28] namely cleaning and polishing footwear left by guests outside their bedrooms, helping with odd jobs around the hotel and transporting luggage. It was a most enjoyable experience greatly enhanced by the kindness and good humour shown to the boys by their direct 'boss', handyman Attie Williamson and his wife Mimie, who was cook. Lessel Allan was the hotel manager.

The lounge bar was a very popular, comfortable place for locals to meet up for a chat by the fire. On the wall opposite the windows was the mural depicting the Sooth End which had been painted by Jim Kerr in the early 1960s at the request of Mr Allan. It was greatly admired by all. A welcoming face behind the lounge bar was Dolly Johnson who, along with her daughter Marjory, who was head waitress in the dining room, provided many years of dedicated service to the hotel. The room attached to the public bar at the rear of the hotel was a popular venue for playing darts.[29]

Over the years many distinguished people, too many to mention individually, have been guests at the hotel including Sir John Betjeman who was Poet Laureate at the time. He afterwards wrote a poem entitled *Shetland*. Other famous guests were Beatle Paul McCartney and his then wife Linda.[30]

Although the gas explosion in 1926 caused some damage to the hotel it was insignificant when compared with the aftermath of the devastating fire that swept through the building during the night of 14th September, 1987, that had started just before midnight. Firefighters fought for over three hours to bring the blaze under control and were praised, as life-saving heroes, after two elderly guests had no hesitation in saying that they owed them their lives. One of these guests was taken to hospital suffering from smoke inhalation and several firefighters too were treated for cuts and smoke injuries. All residents, patrons and staff were safely evacuated but the top three storeys of the hotel were gutted and the lounge bar on the ground floor suffered water damage.[31]

To see the roofless Queens was heartbreaking for many but, like the phoenix, it rose from the ashes and reopened following extensive refurbishment.

Following the death of Alexander I. Tulloch in 1986, the family firm Tulloch of Shetland carried on the business with Neil Wilkins as managing director.

In 1993 the Queens Hotel was sold to J.W.G. plc and became part of the KGQ group incorporating Kveldsro, Grand and Queens Hotels. Kveldsro was sold in 2004 to Brudolff Hotels Group.[32]

The Queens Hotel will be celebrating its 150th anniversary in 2018 and it is hoped that this historic building will continue to provide a service for visitors and locals for many years to come.

95. Re-roofing the building following the fire on 14th September, 1987. December 1987

59 Commercial Street

The Hygienic Snack Bar was a mecca for Shetlanders growing up in the 1950s and '60s as it boasted a horseshoe-shaped serving bar and Shetland's first jukebox, installed in 1953.[1] 'Da HiJinks', as it was most commonly known, was a trendy meeting place where young people hung out, especially in the evenings and on Saturday and Sunday afternoons. In fact, a queue used to form on Sunday waiting for the door to open at 3.00pm. There was great expectation every week to discover what new record had been added to the jukebox, and three that spring to mind are Ricky Nelson and *Hello Mary Lou*, Emile Ford and the Checkmates with *What do ya wanna make those eyes at me for* and Eddie Cochran's *Three steps to Heaven*.[2]

The snack bar was the brainchild of Lillian and Frank Chadwick and the name – The Hygienic – had been coined by Lillian to emphasise the standard she wished to maintain in the premises.[3] It proved to be a very busy and popular establishment, which catered for local folk and visitors as well as teenagers.

The Hygienic occupied a site at 59 Commercial Street, on the corner opposite the Queens Hotel and Old Tolbooth. In earlier times on part of this site stood a triangular shaped building called the Half Nyepkin, so named because of its appearance similar to that of a folded head-square (headscarf). It had been built between 1760 and 1790[4] to fill a space between two buildings on the corner and had been a saddlers and then a shoemaker's shop.[5]

96. *Hygienic Snack Bar advertisement as shown at the North Star Cinema*

97. *From left is the Old Tolbooth, then Queens Hotel with Hay & Company's shop opposite, and the Half Nyepkin. Late 1870s*

98. *On the left is William Brown, grocer. The building extending into Commercial Street at Hay's Corner was Hay & Company's licensed grocer shop which was demolished in 1892 and replaced with the building we see today. The Old Tolbooth is in the background and the Queens Hotel is on the right. c.1885*

The building adjacent to the Half Nyepkin on the south side was that of Peter Innes of Fracafield, merchant. It was built about 1790[6] and sold to James Hay in 1801.[7] It was here that Walter Sinclair, a tenant, established Sinclair's Tavern, the first public house in Lerwick. A shop was at ground level with a billiard room situated in the house at the back.[8] This is where Sir Walter Scott stayed when he visited Shetland in 1814.[9]

This old building that jutted out into Commercial Street became Hay & Company's licensed grocer shop and the area became known as Hay's Corner. In 1892, in response to an appeal by the Commissioners of Police for improvements to the street, Mr Arthur J. Hay, on behalf the company, agreed to demolish the premises and submitted plans for the erection of a new building on the site. Included in the development was the site of the adjacent Half Nyepkin.

The new structure was built in line with the property to the south belonging to Mr William Brown (known as 'Willie Plenty'), grocer at 51 Commercial Street (for several years, until 2016, this was The Spider's Web shop). The street was therefore widened by six feet (1.8m) at the south end of the new building and by four feet (1.22m) at the north end. Made entirely of local stone, complete with turret, the building was two storeys high and consisted of a grocer shop on the ground floor, with handsome plate glass windows on the rounded corner occupying the site of the demolished Half Nyepkin.

On top were offices and a dwelling, with attics above. Mr Henry Sinclair carried out the masonry work with the joinery work completed by Messrs Sinclair and Hardie.[10]

Hay & Co continued in the rebuilt licensed grocer shop at 59 Commercial Street until 1896, when the business was taken over by John Tait who, for many years, had been manager. The Hay family retained ownership of the building. Mr Tait's business was now extended as he also traded at 61-63 Commercial Street selling wines, groceries and provisions. His newly acquired premises became a ship chandlery, stocking fishing material and seamen's clothing, etc.[11] Following Mr Tait's death in 1904, the firm John Tait & Co carried on trading as general merchants until 1914 when John McKay, manager of the Queens Hotel, converted the shop at number 59 to the Queens Hotel Bar.[12] The following year, 61-63 Commercial Street became Messrs J. & J. Tod's store.

In 1922 the Queens Hotel Bar premises was let to Albert Harris, draper, who advertised ladies' high class day and evening gowns, underwear, lingerie, furs, costumes and blouses of the latest fashion.[13]

99. *The steps are in front of the Old Tolbooth. On the left is the Queens Hotel with the newly built premises opposite, at 59 Commercial Street, which replaced Hay & Company's shop and the Half Nyepkin in 1892-93*

The shop was taken over in 1928 by the firm of Inkster & Jamieson, general merchants who also had a shop at 15 Commercial Street (now demolished), previously occupied by Thomas Stout at Stout's Court.[14] Some readers will no doubt remember 59 Commercial Street referred to as Hairy Ned's, the name by which the proprietor, Edward Inkster, was otherwise known. It is recorded that one window displayed a religious tract while the other, for some reason, flaunted a pair of ladies' bloomers. In addition, the shop stocked clocks and watches, fancy goods and confectionery and carried out clock and watch repairs.[15]

The business was carried on by Mr Inkster's son Jim, until Frank and Lillian Chadwick opened the aforementioned Hygienic Snack Bar in May 1952, offering morning coffee, afternoon teas and cooked snacks. The opening times were originally Monday 9.00am-2.00pm; Tuesday to Saturday 9.00am-2.00pm and 3.00pm-9.00pm; and Sunday 3.00pm-9.00pm[16] but were later extended to accommodate passengers arriving by boat. Often the Hygienic remained open until 11.30pm. After it became established, the owners opened the Norven Guest House upstairs, then in 1957 they took over Hayfield Hotel.[17]

In 1962 the snack bar became a café operated by the Queen's Hotel and continued under several owners including Mr John (Jock) Laurie, Mrs Violet Duncan, Mrs Christina Johnson, Mrs Mary Smith until 1981, when it again returned under the control of the Queens Hotel. After opening in 1990 as Arran Aromatics the RNLI acquired the premises in 1993. A charity shop was opened and volunteers raised funds for the institution. When the RNLI moved into the Old Tolbooth in 2005 the next occupant was Merrie Dancers followed by the Lodberrie Deli until December 2016[18] then by From Shetland with Love.

The exterior of the building remains virtually unchanged since it was built in 1892.

100. *Looking towards the entrance to the Snack Bar. On the left is the Life-boat Station, also the Royal Hairdressing Saloons, and on the right is the Old Tolbooth.*

61-63 COMMERCIAL STREET

101. *The much admired white horse model in the window of Mr Levack's saddle shop at 61 Commercial Street. On the left is Hay & Company's shop and the Half Nyepkin which filled the corner space. Late 1870s*

A well-known and greatly admired landmark in Old Lerwick was the model of a white horse which stood in the window of a shop at 61 Commercial Street (now site of Vaila Fine Art), occupied by Mr Levack, saddler, who originated from Caithness.[1]

When the building was restructured a new bank office, that of the North of Scotland Banking Company, opened in the rooms to the left of the front door in 1883.[2] The other end of the building, along with 59 Commercial Street, was Hay & Company's shop and store, managed by John Tait. The bank moved to the foot of Mounthooly Street (now Miller Opticians) about 1894, then Hay & Co occupied the whole building. Mr Tait took over the business in 1896 and traded as John Tait & Co, but the Hay family retained ownership of the building.

Following Mr Tait's death in 1904, the licence for John Tait & Co, general merchants, at 59, 61 and 63 Commercial Street, was granted to John's second son John Murray Tait. Two years later the interior of the building was completely renovated[3] and, in 1909, John moved to Western Australia[4] but the business continued.

In 1914 John McKay, manager of the Queens Hotel, converted the shop opposite the hotel (at 59 Commercial Street) to the Queens Hotel Bar.[5] The following year J. & J. Tod, wholesale provision merchants, took over the remainder of the building as a store.[6]

The premises then became a butcher's shop and served that purpose for almost 80

102. Hay & Company's buildings at 59 and 61 Commercial Street occupied by John Tait & Co. Late 1890s

103. Smith & Co, butchers. Economy Corner is the light coloured building at the foot of Church Lane. Late 1950s

years. The first butcher was Laurence Smith, who obtained the premises as a sub-tenant of J. & J. Tod in June 1920 and opened for business as Smith & Company, fleshers, greengrocers and fruit salesmen. Laurence bought the premises in 1928 from Miss M. E. Hay, Kveldsro, who had inherited the Hay estate.[7]

Laurence Smith sold the building to J. W. Foulis, butcher, Kirkwall, in 1947,[8] who in turn sold to William C. Smith in 1955.[9] In November 1967, the end part of the building at 63 Commercial Street, which included a dairy in the early 1950s, was sold to Zetland County Council[10] and was subsequently demolished during the construction of Church Road. As a consequence the butcher shop also lost its back shop and the council agreed to allow the empty Seaview Stores opposite (at 36 Commercial Street), to be temporarily utilised for their business. The Smith family were decanted to the vacated Simmer Dim Restaurant at 36a Commercial Street until the work was completed the following year.[11]

The shop remained in the Smith family until 1994 when it was sold to Mark Anderson, while Mrs Mary Smith continued to live above at 63a.[12] James McMillan, followed by Laurence Malcolmson, each owned the butchers' shop for a short time until March 1999 when it was sold to Dorota Rychlik and her husband Richard Rowland. Following refurbishment, 61 Commercial Street reopened as Vaila Fine Art.[13]

65 Commercial Street

104. *Smith & Co, the dairy and Economy Corner. Laurence Tulloch is on the left and Bill Smith on the right. Early 1950s*

Another of Lerwick's old buildings was situated at the foot of South Kirk Closs, later Church Lane, and across what is now Church Road. Thomas Strong, born in Dunrossness, was a boot and shoemaker who had established his business in 1845.[1] He bought the building at 65 Commercial Street from the estate of William Hay of Hayfield in 1852. The purchase consisted of a shop, two dwelling houses with shed and back closs, which became Strong's Court, on the southeast side of South Kirk Closs.[2] The family did not live there but in a house at Twageos, to the south of Twageos House, that was later known as Hyslop's Cottage.[3] About 1890, the Strongs moved to the house Glenlea in what is now Ronald Street.[4]

Two of Thomas' sons, John and Thomas, worked with their father[5] and following his death in 1893 it was Thomas who inherited the business selling boots, shoes and slippers, until his death in 1934.[6]

On 1st June, 1935, Laurence Smith, in addition to his butcher shop at 61-63 Commercial Street, opened a new business next door in 65 which he called Economy Corner. It was a general and fancy drapers shop selling Shetland yarns, ladies' hosiery and frocks, underwear, jumpers, scarves, and a wide range of rugs, sheets, bedspreads, towels, tablecloths, cushion covers and other household goods.[7]

The owner of the premises, Thomas Arthur Strong, a nephew of Thomas Strong Jnr. who lived in New Zealand, sold the building along with 2 and 4 Church Lane to Zetland County Council in 1965. These buildings were demolished to allow the construction of Church Road.[8]

The business of Economy Corner carried on for a short time across the street in the former, vacant Seaview Stores.[9]

Seaview Stores and Seaview House

105. *Seaview Stores with Smith & Co opposite. 1950s*

In 1886, when the shore behind the Old Tolbooth was filled in[1] to form the South Esplanade, the Cockstool Rock disappeared under the rubble. This rock was originally Lerwick's landing place. In the mid-1700s there were no piers, houses or lodberries along the shore between there and 10 Commercial Street[2] (often referred to as Patrick Torrie's House).

To the northwest of the Tolbooth, in 1805 James Mouat built premises, including a house, known as Da Cockstool and bordering what is now Commercial Street at No. 36. The shop and office was at street level, with cellar underneath and lodberry behind, opposite the Cockstool Rock.[3] James Mouat was an agent for the Leith traders *Dolphin*, *Magnus Troil* and the *Sisters*.[4]

James's son Peter inherited the property and the tenant of the grocer shop for many years was William Robertson, merchant/tailor and his family. Following William's death in 1863 the business was carried on by his wife Jean and she was followed by their daughter Ann, who ran the shop until emigrating to Australia in 1878.[5]

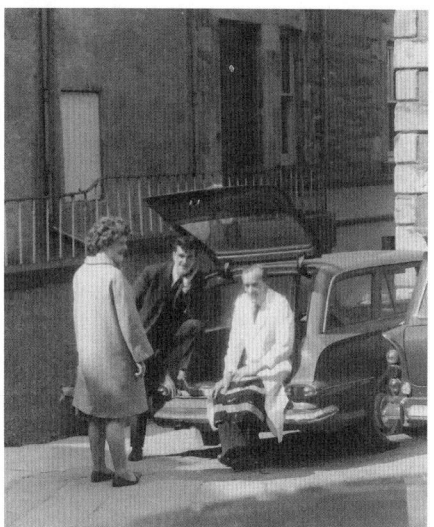

106. *The author and his sister Dorothy with Bill Smith of Smith & Co. Seaview Stores and the entrance to Seaview House are in the background. c.1966*

Capt. William James, china merchant and grocer, then acquired the premises. An interesting event took place on 17th June, 1873, when a local boatman and carpenter was accused of stealing whalebone umbrella ribs from his shop![6] As a result he was imprisoned in Fort Charlotte. Then, in March 1884, a fire destroyed the dwelling house but the business premises was saved. Earlier that day, Capt. James was at Scalloway to join the S.S. *Queen* but he fell in the sea and was almost drowned. He lost a carpet bag. Felix McShane, who was described as his servant, had the keys to the premises and was in charge at the time. When it became known that the building had been highly insured, arson was suspected and both men found themselves arrested,[7] and following a jury trial were sentenced to 18 months in prison.[8]

In 1885 the trustee on behalf of William's creditors sold the property at 36 Commercial Street to Daniel Rendall Williamson,[9] a merchant in Leith who had been born in Yell in 1843. He moved to Lerwick to take over Da Cockstool shop.

The next grocer and general merchant after Daniel Williamson was Robert L. Anderson in 1922.[10]

By 1932 James J. Smith, brother of Laurence who had shops opposite, was at Seaview Stores but it was still referred to by its former name, Da Cockstool, for many years.[11] In the early 1950s the shop was advertised as a grocers, provision and wine merchants offering a prompt delivery service and stocking, among other things, paraffin, a range of feeding stuff for hens and sheep, spirits and beers, some of which was bottled in the cellar.[12]

The Seaview Stores building was sold to Zetland County Council in 1964.[13] For a very short time Economy Corner traded from the vacant building and then it was let, in 1965, to Miss Inger Lie and Miss Joan Anderson who ran a hairdressing business there until 1967.[14] They were followed by William C. Smith, butcher, who that year had sold the end part of his shop at 63 Commercial Street to Zetland County Council for demolition to allow for the construction of Church Road. As a consequence, the butcher shop lost its back shop and during the construction phase permission was given to utilise the empty Seaview Stores for business purposes.

Seaview House

Daniel R. Williamson, who had bought the shop and property at 36 Commercial Street in 1885, built a dwelling house on the site of Mouat's Lodberry in 1896, which he named Seaview House. It was accessible from the street by a walkway along the side

107. *Seaview Stores and Seaview House in May 1968, shortly before demolition. Part of the Old Tolbooth is to the right*

of the shop nearest to the Old Tolbooth. The address was 36a Commercial Street. Daniel died in 1922 at 3 St Magnus Street.

For some years Mrs Christina Eunson (née Deyell), who was a school teacher and headmistress, lived in Seaview House before moving to Leog where she died in 1961. The Simmer Dim Restaurant was opened on the upper floor by Miss Mary Robertson until 1964 when the building was sold to Zetland County Council, but Robert McKay was a tenant for a short time. Mrs C. Anderson was the tenant until 1966.[15]

108. *From left is the Queens Hotel, RNMDSF, Seaview House with Jamieson's Knitwear shop, and the Seamen's Home. 1950s*

109. To allow the newly constructed Church Road to be continued down to join the Esplanade three buildings were demolished – Seaview Stores, Seaview House and the Seamen's Home. The car (centre) is approximately where Economy Corner stood. September 1968

In 1967 the Smith family were decanted to Seaview House while demolition was taking place at their shop at 63 Commercial Street. They returned in 1968 following completion of the work.[16]

The shop underneath Seaview House was accessible from the South Esplanade and leased to tenants over the years. In 1952 Jamieson's Knitwear moved there and remained throughout the 1950s. Then followed Jim Burgess, who sold motor and agricultural spares until about 1967 when the firm moved to 20 Commercial Road.

Seaview Stores and Seaview House were demolished in 1968 to allow the completion of Church Road.

THE OLD TOLBOOTH

110. *An early view of the south end prior to the formation of the South Esplanade*

The word tolbooth, or 'tow böd', simply means a townhouse where tolls (taxes) were collected. They were built throughout Scotland and served as a meeting place for the burgh councils and courts, and for the imprisonment of criminals and debtors.[1]

The history of the Tolbooth in Lerwick begins between 1660 and 1670, when a small structure without a tower was erected, about half the size of the building we see today.[2]

In 1755, when this first Tolbooth was almost 100 years old and in a ruinous condition, the Commissioners of Supply (forerunner of the county council and responsible for the justice in the islands) proposed that the Tolbooth should be enlarged, or replaced by a new building incorporating a prison, as the one in Scalloway Castle was in a state of disrepair (Scalloway was the capital of Shetland at that time). In 1760 Lord Morton, feudal superior of the islands, approved the latter proposal.[3]

After failure to obtain a new site it was decided, in 1766, to retain the existing one. The area was too small for a larger building until Arthur Nicolson of Lochend gifted a small piece of ground, and an adjacent old house belonging to Magnus Fea was purchased and then demolished.[4]

Some of the materials from the old Tolbooth were utilised and some were sold. Thomas Bolt of Bressay was in charge of the work and Robert and James Forbes, both experienced masons, supervised the 785 masons retained. Materials included 356 boatloads of quarried stones from Bressay, 70 boatloads of shell sand from Trebister, and freestone was brought in from Orkney and Leith.[5]

On 3rd June, 1767, the foundation stone was laid with full Masonic honours, the first public appearance by Morton Lodge No. 89 since its inauguration in 1764. After the ceremony, 15 brethren adjourned to Mr William Farquhar's public house where they consumed three bowls of punch to the *"success to the Craft and Work just begun"*.[6] The premises is now incorporated into the Shetland Times Bookshop but was previously the barber shop occupied by Mr William Tait, otherwise known as Feejur.

The new Tolbooth, a two-storey building above a basement, was completed in 1770. The building cost just under £800 and was funded by loans, donations and proceeds of wrecks. A small spire was added two years later.[7] In addition, Morton Lodge pledged a donation of £30 in return for the permanent hire of a room in the east half of the top floor. The first lodge meeting was held in the new venue on 11th September that year.[8] The room was also used as a ballroom and as a meeting place by the Commissioners of Supply.

In addition to the Masonic Lodge/ballroom on the top floor, there were two rooms known as the 'debtors' prison' which were notoriously insecure, in that prisoners were allowed to leave and enter as they wished.

In 1772 John Mowat, previously a criminal in the Tolbooth, was appointed dempster (doomster, the officer of a court of justice who pronounced the sentence) at £10 per annum. The provision of stocks and jougs (an iron collar which was fastened around a prisoner's neck and was attached by a chain to the wall) were considered essential to deter thieves. William Mouat was employed as gaoler at a salary of £2. Peat fires heated parts of the Tolbooth.[9]

In 1779 Mr John Bruce of Sumburgh, collector of customs, requested to use the ballroom as a Custom House and also have the sole use of one of the prison cells. This was agreed but with the proviso that any goods he had stored would be moved when the cell was needed.[10]

There was an outside freestone staircase, adjacent to the present day Queens Hotel, leading up to the Masonic Lodge room. It soon became the centre of entertainment and public balls were frequently held due to the presence of 300 men stationed at Fort Charlotte and the numerous vessels visiting Lerwick Harbour. Incidentally, it was here that Sir Walter Scott, the famous author, was guest of honour during his visit to Shetland in 1814.[11]

The history of the Tolbooth bell is interesting. In 1744 a ship, the *Queen of Sweden*, belonging to the Royal Swedish Asiatic Company, had sunk at South Ness, Twageos. The ship's bell had been presented to the parish of Lerwick as a thanks offering, but it couldn't be used as the Auld Kirk had no steeple. The newly built Tolbooth had a small steeple without a bell, therefore the *Queen of Sweden's* bell, along with another small old bell, was sent south to be recast into a larger one. This new bell had no maker's name, only a government mark – the broad arrow – dated 1782. The Tolbooth steeple was altered to house the bell, which was used for both kirk and public use.[12]

In 1790 Thomas Stout, builder (grandfather of Sir Robert Stout, at one time prime minister of New Zealand), was permitted to build a small shed within the bulwark at the rear of the building.[13]

The courtroom was in the west half of the main floor. In 1817 a room was acquired in the east end for a subscription school and Mr John McMorine was appointed teacher at an annual salary of £80.[14] This room then became a sheriff clerk's office and office for weights and measures in 1828.[15]

The provision of a clock had been overlooked when the small spire was built in 1772. This was remedied in 1825 when a square clock tower, set centrally on the roof ridge, replaced the former. It was stone built and terminated in a simple slated spire above louvered belfry-openings. The clock, costing £20, made by James Clark, Edinburgh and stamped No. 57, was purchased through public subscription and was installed in the tower. It had four convex copper faces and the mechanism allowed for one hand to show the hour. Lerwick now had a 'toon clock'.[16] A minute hand was added later.

111. The stocks were situated in the structure to the right of the entrance to the Tolbooth. Early 1880s

The two cells situated in the basement rejoiced in the name 'thieves' hole'. By all accounts it certainly was a desperate hole. One prisoner described, in 1795, that he was incarcerated without bed or bed clothes, fire or candle or anything to sit or lie on except rubbish and filth of various sorts. The Tolbooth was irreverently known as 'Nicol's Hotel' after Sergeant Nicol, an old soldier who at one time was gaoler.[17]

Attached to the right of the Tolbooth's entrance was a small structure, roofed with flagstones, and it was here that criminals were compelled to sit in the stocks.[18]

112. The stocks as depicted by the artist Fred Irvine

A list of prisoners held in the Tolbooth can be found in Shetland Museum & Archives. It reveals, for example, that in March 1825 John Henderson, a labourer from Lerwick, aged 16, was confined to the stocks following a petty theft conviction.[19]

In 1836 a prison inspector was appalled by the laxity of conditions in the gaol, also the dampness in the basement cells, and he declared the building unfit.[20] Two years later the Sheriff Court and prisoners relocated to Fort Charlotte, although the Tolbooth continued to be occasionally used as a lock-up.

In 1855 there was a tragedy in the Tolbooth. Kirstie Cadell and her three bairns had been evicted from a room in Sooth Kirk Closs (now Church Road) and, having been refused allowances from the parochial board, had been forced to live on a stair-head in the closs, and support themselves by begging. Destitute, she and the bairns sought shelter in the Tolbooth where, suffering from starvation and hypothermia, she died on the inner staircase.[21]

Morton Lodge vacated in 1859 and held meetings in the Auld Kirk in Queens Lane until they purchased that building in 1870.[22] The Lodge still remains at that location.

113. Dutch fishermen waiting for their mail on a Sunday morning. Seaview Stores can be seen in the background. c.1905

In 1875 the County Buildings were built and the sheriff, lawyers and prisoners were transferred from Fort Charlotte. In 1878 the occasionally-used lock up relocated from the Tolbooth to the fort, and this allowed the Post Office to return to the Tolbooth, having previously been there in the 1850s. Initially the main floor was used, with upper rooms occupied by the Shetland Literary and Scientific Society as a library and museum, until it moved into rooms above what is now Faerdie-Maet at 38-42 Commercial Street in 1897. Another upper room was an office for Mr A. J. Garriock, auctioneer and commission agent. Eventually the Post Office occupied the whole building until moving to the present location in 1910.[23]

In 1912 the Tolbooth was completely renovated and the Royal Mission for Deep Sea Fishermen moved in. Two large rooms on the main floor were converted into a meeting room and a place where fishermen could read and write letters. Upstairs were beds where sick or convalescent fishermen could be nursed. In 1922 the Mission purchased the premises and remained there until 1962, apart from a period in 1930 when it temporarily vacated to allow the building to be used as a hospital following an outbreak of scarlet fever in the town.[24]

The whole clock tower was removed in 1927 and stored in the basement of the Town Hall until local businessman Mr Algar Sutherland acquired the structure. In 1965 he incorporated a replica into the newly built roof of Bolt's Garage and Showroom, now the Toll Clock Shopping Centre.[25]

In 1962 Zetland County Council purchased the Old Tolbooth and it became the headquarters of the civil defence.[26] It was even a hall for Up-Helly-A' for five years from 1964. In 1968 it was sublet to the British Red Cross, the WRVS, and Shetland Tourist Association.[27]

The Hoversta Dairy initially operated from the basement[28] and then from part of the extension which had been added along the length of the rear of the building early in

114. *The last mail leaving the Post Office on Sunday, 8th May, 1910. The new Post Office opened the following day, a short distance along the street on the site of Sinclair's Beach*

the 20th century.[29] The dairy ceased in 1963 and the Red Cross opened its charity shop there in 1976. At the other end of the extension was the Lerwick Old People's Welfare Committee rest room, previously occupied by Mr Robert Paton, barber, affectionately known as 'the lightning barber'.[30]

Due to its deteriorating condition, the main building was condemned by the local authority (by now Shetland Islands Council) in 1999. The Red Cross was forced to leave and subsequently relocated to 125-127 Commercial Street.

In 2001 ownership of the Old Tolbooth passed from Shetland Islands Council to Shetland Amenity Trust, and in the same year the building was leased to the RNLI. However the 'pensioners' rest room' was allowed to remain open until July 2003.

In August 2003, Shetland Amenity Trust took possession of the building. The renovation contract was awarded to building contractors DITT, and work commenced in September 2003. The long extension at the rear was removed and a replica clock tower was built into the roof, returning the building to its original appearance.

By 2005 the building was operational; the lifeboat shop moved across into the

115. *One of the original clock faces on display inside the Toll Clock Shopping Centre. 2017*

new premises from 59 Commercial Street, and the headquarters from the adjacent old Hay's Lodberry. In August, contractors DITT Construction scooped the top commercial category prize in the Scottish Master Builder of the Year Awards 2005.[31]

It may be of interest that two artefacts of the Old Tolbooth still exist. The stocks are on show in the Shetland Museum, and one of the clock's convex copper faces survived storage and can be seen on a wall inside the Toll Clock Shopping Centre.

116. *RNLI Lerwick Lifeboat Station. 2017*

Early Schools

117. Clairmont Place, with the Congregational Church shown centre left and the Parochial School directly opposite. The row of houses in the centre are in Mounthooly Street. Late 1880s

The first mention of a school in Lerwick is in 1689. This is interesting given that the first substantial houses were only built about 1640. Mr Walter Innes, signatory to Sasines, in 1678 and 1689 is described in the latter as *"teacher of the gramer schooll at Learwick."*[1] The 'school' was probably just a room in his residence but unfortunately the location was not recorded.

An earlier deed, dated 1634, lists Robert Ramsay as a schoolmaster in Scalloway, which was the capital of Shetland at that time.[2]

Another early teacher was Charles McNab, who was contracted in 1775 by a group of ten subscribers in Lerwick to teach Latin grammar, English, writing, arithmetic, bookkeeping and church music, for a period of three years. His annual salary of £30 included £2.10 shillings (£2.50) from the interest of a bond, courtesy of Thomas Gifford of Busta.[3] Again, the location is unknown.

Another place of learning was the Subscription School, named simply because it was funded by subscription. Andrew Duncan, sheriff-substitute, headed the group of 13 subscribers and the others were merchants and landowners. The school was located in a room provided by Morton Lodge No. 89 in the Tolbooth (now the RNLI headquarters), the only public building in Lerwick at that time. In 1817 John McMorine was appointed teacher at an annual salary of £80. The Rev. John Menzies, the parish minister, had authority over certain aspects of the curriculum and regularly visited the school. Mr McMorine left Shetland in 1823 to continue his theology studies.[4]

Other small subscription and private schools followed. In 1835 one opened in rooms in the Auld Kirk (now part of the Masonic Hall in Queens Lane), and the teacher was a young Englishman belonging to the Moravian sect or United Brethren. He had been educated at a seminary in Saxony, Germany, which was supported by the sect. The school operated for about three years with a number of different teachers, all Moravians, one of whom was a German national.

The following year another school, also using rooms in the Auld Kirk, was opened with provision for 21 pupils. Sixteen subscribers each paid two guineas (£2.10). The first headmaster was Mr W. L. Wünsche, a German Moravian, who received a salary of £80 per annum but he was only in post for a short time. Several assistants replaced him, including John G. Glass who was appointed in 1842.

While Mr Glass occupied part of the building, a Miss Gordon conducted a fairly large infant school in the lower east end of the Auld Kirk. At the same time another subscription school was established in the front room of a house at 6 Mounthooly Street. It was operated by John B. Lyall, assisted by his sister who taught in the infant department. The school later moved to the Auld Kirk for a very short time before closing.

Due to the economic climate in Lerwick by 1844 the number of pupils on the Subscription School roll decreased to nine and it too closed. Fortunately for Mr Glass, the Parochial School was looking for a new headmaster and he was subsequently offered the post.[5] The Parochial School had been established in Lerwick in 1816 and was, like the other parochial or parish schools in Shetland, the result of the efforts of the Society for the Propagation of Christian Knowledge. The Scottish wing (the SSPCK) was created by Royal Charter in 1709 as a separate organisation. The Parochial School was at Clairmont Place, for many years the Baptist manse (now a private residence). Reading, writing, arithmetic, book-keeping, English grammar, mathematics and navigation were taught as the basic courses, with the addition of Latin, Greek, French and German.

However, Mr Glass found the building to be unsuitable and hired two upper rooms in the Auld Kirk, where the school remained until his death in early 1854.[6] His replacement was James Hunter, who relocated the school back to Clairmont Place.

In 1855 the Rev. Andrew MacFarlane of the United Presbyterian Church in Hangcliff Lane (later Emmanuel Christian Fellowship) preached a sermon which ended with an appeal to the young men in the congregation to help educate the many poor children and young people in the town who could not read or write. Six came forward to form the Lerwick Instruction Society, funded solely by donors. Classes were held Monday to Friday in the former subscription rooms in the Auld Kirk for about six years. In 1857 the sum of £10, almost half the total of donations, came from Arthur Anderson, who was born in the Böd of Gremista and co-founded the P&O Shipping Company.[7] It was due to his interest in the society, and his generosity, that the Anderson Educational Institute (Anderson High School) was built. In 1862 the upper school at the AEI was opened on the 4th August, with the elementary classes commencing on the 1st December.

By now it was apparent that the Parochial School at Clairmont Place was too small to meet the needs of the rising population. In 1865 the first buildings of any importance

118. *Parks at the Sletts are in the foreground. Bordering Scalloway Road from left are two houses (Seaview and Johnson Cottage), then the Schoolhouse and Lerwick Public School or 'Calderhead's School'. To its far right is Lerwick Infant School (now the Church of Jesus Christ of Latter-day Saints), with the Methodist Church behind and the Wesley manse. c.1880*

to be constructed in the New Town (the area west of the Hillhead) were the Lerwick Public School and schoolhouse.[8] These were built on what was identified as the Town's Park No. 8, near the junction of what is now King Harald Street and Scalloway Road, at a cost of £60 per acre.[9] The school was built to accommodate 150 pupils.

Most of the children relocated from the Parochial School to the new Lerwick Public School, along with their headmaster, James Hunter. He had been in post since 1854 and he continued as headmaster of the new school. It consisted of one large classroom, a smaller room, and an infants' classroom (presided over by Mrs Hunter), the schoolhouse and garden.[10] However, it was soon commonly called the Parochial School, and then Calderhead's School after the headmaster who followed Mr Hunter.[11]

The former school at Clairmont Place was sold at public auction in 1864 to Sinclair Thomson to provide a place of worship for the small number of Baptists in the town.[12]

In 1868, four years after St Magnus Episcopal Church was built at Greenfield, the schoolhouse/schoolroom was constructed adjacent to the church. It became generally known as Walker's School, after its founder, the Rev. Robert Walker. About 1890 the school was extended and pupils ranged in number from 70 to 112, until its closure in 1929.[13]

There was some light-hearted name calling amongst the schoolboys. Those

119. *St Magnus Scottish Episcopal Church and Schoolhouse. c.1904*

educated at St Magnus Schoolroom were 'Walker's Holy Ghosts' and they taunted 'Calderhead's Caald Tatties' and vice versa. Although Mr Calderhead was only headmaster for a short time (from 1885 until 1889), he left behind a street name – Calderhead's Brae – the section of what is now Union Street between the Lower Hillhead and King Harald Street.[14]

The Education (Scotland) Act 1872 put forward a national system of education whereby locally elected school boards took responsibility for all parochial and church schools. Attendance at school was compulsory until the age of 13 and was not raised to 14 until 1901.[15]

As a consequence of the Act, in August 1874, Lerwick School Board acquired a site near the Methodist Church. Work began on constructing the Lerwick Infant School (now the Church of Jesus Christ of Latter-day Saints),[16] and it opened on Monday, 7th August, 1876, with a roll of 85 children.[17]

Infant School Brae later became Prince Alfred Street. Miss Janet Gulland, a leading light in the local women's suffrage movement, was the first headmistress and she continued in the service of the school board for 38 years.[18]

The opening of Lerwick Central Public School in 1902 was an important event in that, along with Lerwick Infant School, rooms in the Rechabite Hall in Mounthooly Street, Calderhead's School at the south end of King Harald Street, and St Magnus Schoolroom, there was sufficient provision for primary education for the town's children.[19] This left the Central and the Institute to provide secondary education and the Institute to become a purely secondary school.[20] Before the Central opened (now Islesburgh Community Centre), pupils progressed from Calderhead's School to the Lower School at the Anderson Educational Institute at the age of nine or ten.[21]

In 1908, due to gross overcrowding, Calderhead's School was extended and the

120. *c.1905*

following year it reopened as the new Infant School[22] (later called the Old Infant School, now Lerwick Pre-school).

The former school in Prince Alfred Street then closed and the building was sold to The Independent Order of Good Templars.[23] (The building later became The Shetland Times print works[24] and is now, as previously mentioned, the Church of Jesus Christ of Latter-day Saints.)

Over the years, education provision in Lerwick continued to flourish despite the interruption of two wars. During the Second World War the Institute was commandeered for use as a military hospital and pupils were accommodated in the Central.[25]

The Infant School soon became too small despite the building of huts in the playground to provide additional classrooms. In 1955 work commenced on constructing an infant department at Bell's Brae and the new school opened in June 1957. Upper primary children were taught at what now became known as the Old Infant School and in some ground floor rooms at the Central.[26]

121. *Looking towards Lerwick Central Public School from the Town Hall. c.1905*

In February 1962, work began on the building of an extension to the Anderson Educational Institute. The completed building, officially opened in May 1964, could accommodate 365 pupils and 24 members of staff and replaced the temporary wooden classrooms. The old school was renovated and in effect became a wing of the new school, connected by a covered bridge at first floor level. Two teachers' houses and a house for a janitor were included in the scheme. [27]

In 1967 the Scottish Education Department approved the establishment of a comprehensive school for Lerwick and junior high schools in seven rural areas.

The amalgamation of the Anderson Educational Institute and Lerwick Central Public School took place in 1970 when the Central closed and the Institute became Anderson High School.

Lerwick Primary School was enlarged in 1974, and was officially renamed Bell's Brae Primary School in 1977 when a new primary school was built at Sound.[28]

A large extension was completed at Anderson High School in 1980, which greatly increased classroom accommodation, and by 1983/84 the roll had reached 1,045. In 1984 the two-year secondary course offered at Brae was increased to a four-year course and this reduced the pressure on Anderson High School. Also, that same year saw the completion of a new further education centre on the Anderson High site and the erection of the leisure centre at Clickimin.[29]

The construction of the new Anderson High School at Clickimin commenced in August 2015 and opened in October 2017.

The 1900 Storm

122. *The South Esplanade after the storm. The building on the left is the public toilet and behind it is the Seamen's Home. To its right are a building at Sinclair's Pier, Sinclair's Lodberry and Leask's Lodberry. Behind the barricade are two buildings which were demolished to provide sites for Ellesmere House in 1906 (D. & G. Leslie), and Victoria Building in 1905 (now the site of TSB). 1900*

The great storm of Friday, 16th February, 1900, caused havoc across Shetland but worst hit was the east coastline from Sumburgh to Unst. During the previous days the weather had deteriorated, bringing snow showers with strong southerly wind. By Friday morning the wind had increased to near hurricane force, wet snow was falling and a heavy sea was running from the southeast. The tide was at its height just before noon and Lerwick's south end bore the brunt of the tremendous power of the sea.

Gillie's Pier (opposite the Old Manse gate) had been completely destroyed during the night and Stout's Pier nearby was washed away to within a few feet of Commercial Street. People living on the lower side of the street were evacuated.

The lower parapet wall at the Craigie Stane, believed to have been one of Lerwick's oldest landmarks, collapsed under the pressure. The Lodberrie was damaged and the sea broke over Commercial Street in front of Quendale House.

Part of the sea wall adjoining the Queens Hotel was swept away and huge waves and stones smashed the windows of a house at the south side of Chromate Lane, flooding the rooms. The windows of several houses had to be barricaded. Waves carried boulders and seaweed across the whole of Commercial Street from Leog to the Queens Hotel until it resembled a beach.

The South Esplanade was severely damaged due to the violent sea sweeping in and

123. On the left is the Old Tolbooth, then Seaview House, the Seamen's Home, and where the Post Office now stands, formerly Sinclair's Beach. 1900

meeting the backwash from Victoria Pier. (It may be helpful to know that the breakwater did not exist at this time and, in fact, it was built in 1915 to provide shelter and to protect the pier and South Esplanade from such storms.) Part of the wall bordering the South Esplanade collapsed, a wooden coal store was completely demolished and rooms in the Seamen's Home (demolished in 1968 to make way for Church Road) were flooded. Nearby houses and cellars also flooded and some occupants had to be rescued through windows.

The north end of the town and harbour was relatively unscathed although some workshops, sheds and stables sustained damage. Chimney cans and slates were blown off roofs.

However, Clickimin suffered badly. The newly erected concrete sea defence wall at the Ayre was swept away and the sea carried rubble into the loch. Part of the road here was washed away leaving the main water pipe from the Sandy Loch exposed and the town without a supply for some time.[1]

The dykes along the seafront from the Sletts to Seafield were decimated. Great quantities of haddocks, ling and even a lobster were picked up along the shore.

The following day the wind continued to blow from the southeast and the extent of the damage became apparent. The Street was covered with debris, slush and piles of snow that had fallen from roofs. Barricades were erected at each end of the gap in the sea wall at the South Esplanade and the clean-up began.

124. The Sea Road from in front of what is now Taing House, looking towards Lerwick. Dykes from the Sletts to Seafield were decimated during the storm. 1900

Surprisingly, there were no reported injuries in the town but at the height of the storm a Bressay man was swept away by a tremendous sea and was drowned.

Concern for the safety of the *St Giles*, which had been making her way north, was allayed when news came through that she had docked at Scalloway. Two boats had been carried away, the bridge was partially smashed and other damage had been sustained but the crew and passengers were all safe.[2]

DA AULD KIRKYARD

125. *Da Auld Kirkyard with Queens Lane on the left*

In 1885, when workmen were digging a foundation for Krinigill (the house opposite the Masonic Hall), they found several coffins. This was hardly surprising given that the area was Lerwick's first cemetery, which officially dates back to 1688.[1] However, a gravestone dated 1684 remained in the kirkyard until the 1960s.[2] This kirkyard was established when the town of Lerwick was still part of the parish of Tingwall, and it is known that many of the townsfolk were buried there.[3] The parish of Lerwick came into existence in 1701.[4]

Over the years, ordinary folk were buried alongside prominent people such as merchants, landowners, clergy and some high-ranking Freemasons on the site of what is now the car park between Queens Lane and Church Road. The cemetery became known as Da Auld Kirkyard.

Many interesting individuals, too numerous to list here, had the cemetery as their resting place but one is worthy of mention. In an unmarked site lay Barbara Pitcairn, who has been widely written about due to her secret marriage to John Gifford, the heir to the Busta Estate. She was forced to leave Busta and came back to Lerwick to live in family property at 97 Commercial Street (presently Smiths of Lerwick), where she died in 1766.[5]

The first kirk in Lerwick was built between 1660 and 1670 on the site of the present Masonic Hall. In 1685, in the presence of Robert Ramsay the preacher, one Hendry Smith requested burial space inside the kirk for himself and heirs between those graves of William Adamson and Laurence Sutherland and permission was granted by the Session.[6] In 1688 the building was repaired and a petition from Lerwick residents was presented to the Presbytery of Shetland requesting permission to have a kirkyard surrounding the kirk.[7] This was created between North Kirk Closs (now Queens Lane) and South Kirk Closs (renamed Church Lane in 1845, now Church Road). The discovery of the coffins in 1885 confirmed that the kirkyard surrounded the kirk and it is believed to have extended down the hill for some distance.

During 1782 the kirk was enlarged. This was achieved by building around the existing smaller one, and now forms part of the present Masonic Hall. It would seem that the congregation continued to worship while the work was being undertaken as people brought stools with them to sit on. These were left in the kirk until pews or seats were installed four years later.

In 1815 the kirk was declared to be too small, as the population of Lerwick had increased and 110 families were without seats. The woodwork was decaying and the gallery was in a dangerous condition. A conflict then arose between the Presbytery and the Heritors (proprietors of land or houses) which lasted for five years. The Heritors refused to enlarge the building by 9 feet (2.75m) at each end, as requested by the Presbytery. In 1820 the Court of Session agreed with the sheriff-substitute's report that the kirk should be made large enough to hold two-thirds of the population of the parish, which amounted to 953 persons or, alternatively, a new church to be built with the Heritors meeting the cost.

It was found impossible to enlarge the kirk and in 1825 work commenced on a new building.[8] Lerwick Parish Church opened for worship in 1829 (100 years later it was named St Columba's). The Auld Kirk was converted and used over the years for a variety of purposes such as providing accommodation for a school and also a place of worship for the congregation of St Magnus before their church was built in 1864.

In 1859 Lodge Morton moved to the building but did not purchase it until 1870.[9] Parts were let to other tenants such as the Oddfellows, Good Templars, Salvation Army, Brethren and the Lerwick Club. Weddings, dances and public sales were also held. An office was provided for the Inspector of Poor, which later became a meeting place for the School Board. An old lock-up was situated at the back of the room. *The Shetland Advertiser*, *The Shetland Times* and other publications were also printed in the building.[10]

The kirkyard was used until 1834 when a new cemetery bordering Bullet Loan (now Knab Road) was opened. However, the occasional burial still took place and the last person to be laid to rest in Da Auld Kirkyard was 14-year-old Mary Sandison in 1841.[11]

In a letter to the editor of *The Shetland Times* in 1893, the writer describes his encounters with two young boys who were frequently seen climbing over the kirkyard wall laden with bags containing bones. From an overheard conversation he learned that they were selling these to the ragman "for a half-penny per pound".[12]

Over many decades the kirkyard became neglected, overgrown, and was an increasing embarrassment as it had become a dumping ground, with all manner of refuse having been thrown over the walls.[13]

126. *The top of Queens Lane and Church Lane before Church Road was constructed. c.1960*

In 1961 there was an urgent need to open up a route from the Esplanade to the Hillhead, in order to ease the ever-increasing traffic congestion on the Esplanade.[14] The question was 'how could it be achieved?' The answer was the construction of a road to replace Church Lane, but this would entail the demolition of some shops and several houses, and the Auld Kirkyard becoming part of the development.

Morton Lodge duly sold Zetland County Council a drying green immediately to the east of the Masonic Hall to enable construction of the road, while at the same time the Lodge bought part of the kirkyard directly behind the building. While this purchase provided room for further development, the Lodge was to lose a visible connection with its own history: for over 100 years meetings had been held, often within feet of the graves of earlier Masons.[15]

127. *Demolishing the old houses in Church Lane*

Amazingly, there was no public outcry to the removal of the cemetery, only objections to one-way traffic being introduced in Queens Lane![16] On 15th April, 1966, a heading appeared in *The Shetland Times*: 'Old Kirkyard – Exhumations Approved'. It reported that the Shetland Church of Scotland Presbytery had no observations to make about the proposals, intimated by the Secretary of State, for converting the old cemetery in Queens Lane for part of the new road and car park, providing the removal of remains was carried out decently, as promised by the authorities.[17]

A notice placed in *The Shetland Times* by the county clerk on 13th May, 1966, intimated how the intended transfer of remains should be carried out. A list of the people buried in the kirkyard, derived from gravestones where possible, should be compiled and would be available for inspection at the County Buildings. Relatives could make private arrangements for the re-interment of the deceased person; otherwise, all identifiable remains would be buried at the council's expense in separate graves.[18] Almost 70 inscriptions were recorded.[19]

It would appear that no descendant or representative came forward. To the casual observer the method of removal of the remains could hardly be described as 'decent' as requested by the Presbytery. A number of the very old gravestones were completely shattered under the wheels of the heavy trucks that transferred bones, many in rubbish bags, for burial in the current cemetry at the Knab. Workmen bitterly complained that when handling the bones they weren't even issued with rubber gloves.

Despite the fact that many of the remains were those of respected and prominent citizens with gravestones, they were unceremoniously placed in a communal unmarked grave (now the raised area in the centre of the 1834 cemetery). Of the numerous inscribed gravestones or tablets in Da Auld Kirkyard, only 19 were saved and taken to this cemetery where they were cemented in a row inside the entrance. Reliable eyewitnesses remember that earth containing fragments of bones was taken both to the upper section of the current cemetery at the Knab to create new terraces, and to the town's refuse dump. A reliable source stated that a man was seen at night in the Auld Kirkyard searching for rings and other valuables.[20] Some remains were untouched and are said still to lie under the car park tarmac.

The truth of the matter is that many of the bones had dissolved due to the chemical reaction with the peat present in the soil. However, a very interesting discovery was made during the exhumations. A large pit was unearthed containing a layer of bones covered with straw. It was supposed that this communal interment might have been the result of

128. *Clearing the Auld Kirkyard with St Olaf's Hall in the background*

129. Inside the Old Cemetery, Knab Road, stand the 19 gravestones which were removed from Da Auld Kirkyard

an outbreak of some infectious disease, possibly smallpox.[21]

In 1966 work commenced on building Church Road and car park, at a cost of £20,500 for the first phase, and £19,000 the following year. The road was ready for use by 1968.

Evidence of the existence of the original parish kirkyard are the 19 gravestones now in the old cemetery in Knab Road.[22] In addition, in front of the Masonic Hall, small crosses cut into some of the flagstones can be seen and these marked the site of old graves. It is unfortunate that care was not taken when these were lifted some years ago. Although the graves were left undisturbed, many of these flagstones were not replaced in their original positions over the graves.

130. The flagstone marked with a cross outside Krinigill, opposite the Masonic Hall. 2017

131. *The top of Queens Lane and Church Road. 2017*

132. *Church Road car park, the site of Da Auld Kirkyard. 2017*

DA BIG KIRK

133. *Lerwick Parish Church. Early 1900s*

In 1815, despite the fact that Lerwick Parish Kirk, situated between Nort Kirk Closs and Sooth Kirk Closs (now the Masonic Hall flanked by Queens Lane and Church Road) had been enlarged in 1782, it was considered to be too small. The sheriff-substitute reported that, during the previous 20 years a total of 70 new houses had been built which had increased the population of Lerwick to 2,265, leaving 110 families without seats in the church. Furthermore the woodwork was decaying and the gallery was in a dangerous condition. As is mentioned in the previous chapter, a conflict then arose between the Presbytery and the Heritors which lasted for five years, with the Heritors refusing to enlarge the building at each end as requested by the Presbytery. In 1820 the Court of Session agreed with the sheriff-substitute's report that the kirk should be made large enough to accommodate 953 persons, which was two-thirds of the population of the parish over 12 years of age or, alternatively, a new church should be built with the Heritors meeting the cost. It proved impossible to enlarge the kirk and therefore, after some delay, work commenced in 1825 on the new Lerwick Parish Church at the foot of Knab Road.[1] (It was named St Columba's in 1929.)

It is not known who designed the kirk, but it is recorded that the timber used arrived in Lerwick on 18th August, 1827, on the brig *Elrick* from Miramichi, New Brunswick, Canada. The builder was Robert Stout along with his son William and another mason from Aberdeen, and they hewed all the dress stone in the building. Robert was also the father of Thomas Stout, shopkeeper, whose son was Sir Robert Stout, successively prime minister and chief justice of New Zealand. The family lived at Stout's Court at the south end of Commercial Street.[2]

By 24th December, 1828, the church was completed and on 22nd March, 1829, the first service was held. The preacher was the Rev. Thomas Barclay, who was minister of the parish until he moved south to Peterculter in 1843.[3]

He was followed by the Rev. John Morgan and during his ministry a manse for the parish was built and was completed in 1852.[4] Today it is Clumlie, a private residence at 11 Greenfield Place, Lerwick.

In 1866 the General Assembly of the Church of Scotland lifted its ban on instrumental music in churches. Previously praise had been led by precentors. The kirk session decided to obtain an organ in January 1871. The required sum of just over £300 was quickly raised by subscription and the proceeds of a bazaar. A very fine organ was duly built by Bryceson, Bros & Co, London. Lerwick Parish Church was said to be the second in the whole Church of Scotland to install a pipe organ.[5]

A church improvement scheme initiated in 1885 enabled the kirk session in 1894 to erect an apse, enlarge the organ by adding another key board and eight stops, build a new vestry and session room, install a heating system, modernise the seating arrangements, redecorate the church inside and provide a new pulpit. A church in Gulberwick was also built. The total cost of the project was £2,080.[6]

134. *The Parish manse – Clumlie. c.1904*

John M. Aitken was the main contractor for the alterations to the church and Sinclair & Hardie undertook joiner work. During the renovations the congregation decanted for six months to the Methodist Church, while St Olaf's Free Church provided room for the Sunday school. Special reopening services were held on 10th November, 1895.[7]

135. *The large house on the left is Clumlie, then St Magnus Scottish Episcopal Church and Schoolhouse, Kveldsro Cottage, the Rectory, the rear of Kveldsro House with greenhouse, Greenrig House and Upper Leog on the right. In the immediate foreground is Lovers Loan*

136. The interior before the stained glass windows were added in the 1890s

Individuals also made valuable contributions. Robert P. Gilbertson, donor of the Gilbertson Park, gave a communion table. Others presented communion chairs, the reading desk and the cushion for the pulpit bible.[8] The baptismal font, made of white stone from Caen in France, was also gifted.[9]

The two stained-glass windows in the apse were added in the late 1890s. Miss Elizabeth Spence, Lerwick, gifted the one on the left, while the other was paid for by various members of the congregation and friends.[10]

In 1897 the Dutch Reform Marine Churches in Scheveningen requested that the Rev. L. van der Valk be sent to Shetland to provide advice and assistance to the fishermen. It would appear that he visited the islands on at least four occasions. In June 1897, *The Shetland News* reported that morning and evening services for the Dutch fishermen were conducted in Lerwick Parish Church with the Rev. van der Valk in attendance. Almost a thousand men were present at the evening service, and the proceedings were witnessed by several interested, and no doubt curious, townspeople. On the Saturday and Sunday, 125 Dutch vessels were in Lerwick Harbour, which was the largest number for many years.[11]

While Lerwick Parish Church was being redecorated in 1923 the congregation worshipped in St Clement's Church Hall.[12] Also that year, on 13th May, two memorial tablets listing members of the congregation who had fallen in the First World War were unveiled by the Very Rev. Dr Smith, of Partick, Glasgow, moderator of the General Assembly.[13] A third tablet was added following the end of the Second World War.

On 5th and 7th April, 1929, services were held to celebrate the centenary of the opening of the church.[14] Another event occurred that year resulting in the 'big kirk' receiving a name. A national church union in 1900 between the Free Church (St Olaf's) and the United Presbyterian Church (St Ringan's) resulted in two United Free churches in Lerwick.[15] When the national union of the Church of Scotland with the United Free Church took place in 1929, it was necessary for the 'big kirk' to adopt a name and, from those suggested – St Columba, St Paul and St Ronald – the first was chosen and Lerwick Parish Church was renamed.[16]

In September 1931, St Ringan's and St Olaf's united as one congregation of the Church of Scotland and for a time worshipped alternately in each building until St Ringan's Church was chosen to be used by the united congregation.

The sections of congregation of St Ringan's Church and St Olaf's Church that had elected, in 1929, to adhere to the United Free Church, formed a separate congregation – the Lerwick United Free Church (Continuing). They worshipped in the Rechabite Hall (now Chapel House in Mountooly Street) until 1932 when the congregation moved to the vacant St Olaf's Church and renamed it Lerwick United Free Church.[17]

Fast-days was an ancient custom in the whole Church of Scotland. These were observed in May and November on the Thursday prior to Communion Sunday. The custom grew in Lerwick until the town observed the fast-day as a public holiday and a day of recreation, while an evening service was held at which new communicants were admitted to full membership of the church. By 1939 the observance of fast-days was declining and the kirk session discontinued the practice.[18]

A proposal was adopted by the kirk session in 1955 that there should be a union between St Columba's, Bressay and St Ringan's & St Olaf's Church of Scotland. Following voting by the three congregations this was carried through and the United Charge became Lerwick & Bressay Parish Church.[19]

In 1958 church buildings were exchanged. The Lerwick United Free Church congregation moved from St Olaf's, where they had worshipped since 1932, to the vacant St Ringan's Church building and it regained its old title of St Ringan's United Free Church.[20] The Parish Church obtained St Olaf's building, which was altered with the removal of pews and renamed St Olaf's Hall. It was used for Sunday school, youth activities and church purposes.[21]

During 1986-1987 the congregation was decanted to St Ringan's United Free Church and were welcomed by the congregation while extensive renovations were undertaken, largely financed by a bequest by the late Miss E. Hilda Ganson. A service of rededication was held on Sunday, 3rd May, 1987.[22]

(Incidentally, St Ringan's closed in 1997 and reopened in 2002 as Shetland Library and Learning Centre.)

The 150th anniversary of Lerwick Parish Church was celebrated as was the 175th in 2004 when events were held throughout the summer culminating in a special service in September.

In 2007, as a consequence of spiralling running costs, it was decided to sell St Olaf's Hall with the proceeds going to refurbishing St Columba's. Later that year the hall was bought by a group of local businessmen and was converted to provide up-market offices and residential flats.[23]

The church closed for renovation following the service on Sunday, 2nd March, 2008. The congregation yet again decanted, this time to Lerwick Town Hall where services were held while, in St Columba's, Irvine Contractors carried out rewiring and installed a new heating system. The sloping ground floor was levelled, pews were removed to be replaced with comfortable chairs, and a multi-purpose room, kitchen and toilets were created.[24]

The service of rededication was held on Thursday, 15th January, 2009.[25]

St Clement's Church Hall

———•———

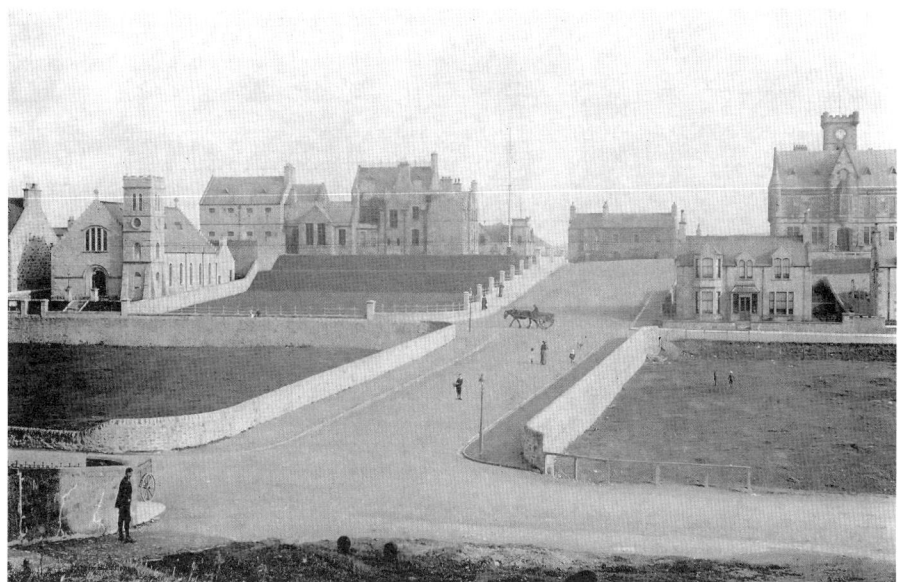

137. *On the left is St Clement's Hall, the Dutch Mission Church, which was built in 1911*

The initiative to erect a building to provide a hall for Lerwick Parish Church, and also premises for Dutch and other foreign fishermen to worship in, was largely due to the efforts of Miss Grace Margaret Turnbull-Stewart of the Old Manse, Lerwick, who was the first president of the church's women's guild. Work began in 1909, with Mr T. L. Bruce, architect, and Mr Peter Thomson, contractor; his tender being £1,615.[1]

St Clement's Church Hall was formally opened on 17th May, 1911, by the Rev. A. J. Campbell for use by Dutch fisherman as a Mission Church.[2] It was described as having seating for about 450 people. The pews were of varnished white wood, while the pulpit and choir platform were pine. A wood lining ran around the walls of the church to the height of four feet (1.22m). The high wooden roof was supported by pitch pine rafters on stone corbels.[3]

A stained glass window was presented to the building committee of St Columba's Church by the Dutch Reformed Churches in the fishing towns along the coast in Holland, as an expression of gratitude for the kindness shown by Lerwick Parish Church to the Dutch fishermen in the past. It was ordained on 2nd July, 1911, by Dom. S. Datema and G. H. van de Vegte, who were in Lerwick providing services to the

Dutch fishermen.[4] The hall provided facilities for the men to worship, rest and write letters to family back home. Plymouth Brethren fishermen, mostly from the Moray Firth area, also used it for several summers.

A tablet to the memory of Miss Turnbull-Stewart was put up in the hall by her fellow guildswomen in recognition of her guild work, her effort in getting St Clement's built and the legacy she had bequeathed. She had died in 1907.

While Lerwick Parish Church was being redecorated in 1923 the congregation worshipped in St Clement's.[5]

During the Second World War the hall had been commandeered by the government and became a first aid post and gas cleansing station.[6] When 6 Hillhead (currently Shetland Family History Society) was requisitioned for ARP (Air Raid Precautions) purposes, the Child Welfare Centre was temporarily relocated to the first aid post at St Clement's Hall.[7] In 1946 it transferred back and remained there until 1971.

War-damage compensation money was used to level the sloping floor in the main part of the hall where pews had been. With the decline of Dutch fishermen visiting Lerwick, St Clement's was utilised for church activities such as Sunday school, congregational meetings, church concerts, Women's Guild meetings and for youth purposes such as badminton.[8] Life Boy meetings were held in the hall from 1948 until 1966.[9]

The Islesburgh Summer Exhibition, 'Shetland Past and Present', was staged in the building annually from 1957 until 1966.[10] Previous exhibitions had been held in Islesburgh House from 1947. The exhibition depicted the old Shetland way of life with demonstrations of spinning, knitting and weaving, and included were displays of crofting and fishing life, model ships and photographs. Following a public request *"for tools, implements, articles of furniture or anything connected with the old way of life in Shetland"* the response was such that by 1957 a larger venue was required and St Clement's was available.

When the Shetland Museum and Library opened in 1966, most items were handed over and the exhibition returned to Islesburgh House and reverted to its original title 'From Ewe to You'.[11]

Badminton players in Lerwick had been seeking premises for some time and that same year Lerwick Town Council agreed to buy St Clement's Hall from the Church of Scotland and lease it to an association as a badminton hall. The St Clement's Badminton Association was accordingly formed. The hall was available every night which meant that more competitive games could be played and this resulted in more people taking up the sport. The hall was also the venue for inter-county matches with Orkney. Competitive badminton continued to be played until facilities became available at Brae School and Clickimin Leisure Centre in the mid-1980s.[12]

St Clement's was an Up-Helly-A' hall from 1968 until 1989.[13]

The building, given a category C(S) listing in August 1996,[14] was used by visiting traders, including Chris Hodge, for regular sales then stood empty for some years until 2011 when Shetland Islands Council decided to sell the property. It was bought by local businessman Malcolm Younger early in 2014, but before he could convert the building to include offices and a photographic studio it was badly damaged by fire, deliberately started by intruders, in October of that year.[15] The following December one of the perpetrators was given a custodial sentence.[16]

St Clement's Hall was later sold and is presently in private ownership.

The Church of Scotland Canteen

At 11.00am on Sunday, 3rd September, 1939, Prime Minister Neville Chamberlain announced on the radio that Great Britain was at war with Germany. In Shetland the naval reservists were first to be called up. The Shetland Defence Company was formed but before the end of the year regular units were beginning to arrive. They included Royal Artillery, Royal Engineers, Royal Army Medical Corps, Royal Signal Corps, and infantry contingents from the Black Watch, Gordon Highlanders and Highland Light Infantry and were stationed in and around the town.[1] Shetland became what was known as a protected area. With an ever-present threat of paratroop landings, as well as possible invasion from the sea, the number of troops in the islands grew until they reached over 20,000.[2]

Consequently, in and around Lerwick several army camps sprung up such as those at Twageos, the Knab, Middlebie Hill (Hayfield), Gilbertson Park and the Circus Camp in what is now the George V Playing Fields.[3]

Sandbags surrounded important buildings, while some were requisitioned for medical and military purposes.[4] One example was the Church of Scotland's St Clement's Hall on St Olaf Street, which was used as a first aid post and gas cleansing station.[5]

138. *St Clement's Hall on the left then the Church of Scotland canteen. In the foreground is the Circus Camp. 1946*

139. *The County Library. c.1950*

Adjacent to the hall a Church of Scotland canteen for members of the armed forces was erected in December 1939 and it was greatly used. Local women volunteers worked in the canteen and, in addition, country parishes were asked to send contributions of home-bakes for the tea tables.[6]

The Rev. George W. Baird was the padre of the canteen in 1942-43 and soldiers of the 2nd Cameron Highlanders came in every day to enjoy a cup of tea, have a sing-song round the piano and receive warm hospitality. He also recalled that in 1966, while on holiday, he met Regimental Sergeant Major Paterson, who was also on holiday, and they talked of their time together in Lerwick. On one occasion the Sergeant Major took over the canteen for band practice and a quiet Sunday afternoon was shattered by the skirl of the pipes and the beat of the drums.[7]

In January 1947, the Zetland County Council Education Committee bought the redundant 'forces canteen' from the Church of Scotland and converted it into the County Library. In July 1948 the existing library, situated above what is now Faerdie-Maet at 42-44 Commercial Street, moved to the new headquarters with Mr George Longmuir appointed as county librarian. In August, Mr E. S. Reid Tait, last president of the Shetland Literary and Scientific Society, formally opened the new premises.[8] The library continued at this location until February 1966 when it moved to the purpose-built Shetland Museum and Library on Lower Hillhead.[9]

Thereafter the old library building was used by small scale industries[10] until it was demolished to provide part of the site of King Erik House, which was built in 1992.

EARLY LERWICK INNS AND HOTELS

Lerwick has had many inns, boarding houses and hotels over the years. They frequently opened and closed as they changed hands, and census records reveal that there were boarders in many houses but too numerous to list here. It is fortunate that a number of distinguished and important people visited Lerwick and wrote about their experience in books or journals. It is difficult to accurately date when establishments offering accommodation were in operation, but the following have been identified on or near Commercial Street during the 19th century.

John Mullay had a lodging house in the Old Manse in the late 1850s, as did John Smythe in Stout's Court.[1]

The first hotel that springs to mind is the Queens Hotel, situated as it is at the south end of Lerwick, visible from the sea and well photographed. It came into existence in 1868 when several buildings, namely houses, shops, offices and lodberries, were combined by Mr George H. B. Hay to form the hotel. It was extended in 1910.

Opposite the Queens Hotel (on the site of what was until 2016 the Lodberrie Deli, then From Shetland with Love), was Sinclair's Tavern[2] where Sir Walter Scott stayed when he visited Shetland in 1814 and slept on a straw couch.[3] It was believed to be the first hotel to be established in Lerwick, complete with a billiard room, and was operated by Walter Sinclair who came from the West Side.[4] Samuel Hibbert arrived in Shetland in 1818 to undertake a geological survey and he commented that an inn called The Lerwick Tavern was kept by a Sinclair family and it *"possesses very good accommodation"*.[5] In 1892 Hay & Company, who owned this property which contained a licensed grocer shop, demolished the block and erected the present building on the site.[6]

140. *The Queens Hotel taken after the extension was built in 1910 but before the breakwater was constructed in 1914-15*

It must be remembered that accommodation often consisted of a box bed, but John T. Reid was taken aback in 1867 to discover that he was being offered space in a two-tiered box bed and would possibly have to share with another occupant. Instead he found comfortable quarters with a Mrs Slater.[7] The Slater family and their boarders are listed at 49 Commercial Street (until 2015 the Magpie's Nest) in the 1871 census.

Thomas Manson suggests that there was a temperance hotel at 67 Commercial Street, in the block at the junction of South Kirk Closs (now Church Road) with the street.[8] Shetland Antiques & Collectables presently occupies the ground floor of this building.

The Zetland Hotel at 77 Commercial Street (now The Shetland Times Bookshop) was run by John O'Brien and his wife Margaret. Here, in 1860, Dr Stephan de Djunkowsky, Apostolic Prefect for the Arctic Region, arrived from Kirkwall to baptise one of the O'Brien children and, at the same time, convert as many people as possible to the Catholic faith.[9] After a very short period in Lerwick he was succeeded by a Belgian priest called Theophilus Verstraeten, who acquired the hotel in which he built a chapel. His time was short-lived as, unfortunately, he contracted smallpox and died in 1871.[10] The premises then ceased to be a hotel and the Catholic Church sold the building. Mr Andrew Smith thereafter operated a licensed grocer shop.[11]

Following Christian Ployen's visit to Shetland in 1839, he wrote that on his arrival in Lerwick he was accommodated in a very good inn called The Lerwick Hotel, which was very superior to other accommodation of the kind.[12] He went on to comment that even the staircases of the inn where he was lodging were carpeted.[13] This establishment is Smiths of Lerwick, at 97 Commercial Street. William Merrylees was listed at that address as inn keeper in the 1841 census.

Mrs Lilias Greig Crutwell opened a private hotel opposite the Masonic Hall in 1888, at 7 Queens Lane (Krinigill), and is recorded as a hotel proprietor there in 1891. An advertisement in *The Shetland Times* a year earlier stated that Mrs Crutwell provided *"board for gentlemen during the winter on Moderate Terms"*.[14] She is recorded in the 1881 census as a private lodging house keeper residing at 2 Hangcliff Lane. She was the grandmother of the late Dr T. Mortimer Y. Manson.

Mrs Margaret Stewart (grandmother of Miss Nancy Stewart, who for many years was a teacher at Lerwick Central Public School) kept a boarding house at 3 Hangcliff Lane. It was there in 1887 that Mr Alexander Coutts and his wife arrived from Aberdeen and took lodgings before moving to accommodation in the newly built Shetland Combination Poorhouse (later Brevik House), where Mr Coutts had been appointed governor.[15]

The Grand Hotel has dominated Lerwick's skyline since it was built in 1886 and is the only early hotel that is still carrying out the function for which it was constructed.

Following the death of Joseph Leask in 1882, two of his nephews, Thomas and Charles, took over his shop at the bottom of Pitt Lane (now R. W. Bayes and the part immediately above). The ambitious brothers soon set their sights on the adjacent ruins of 'Thomas Stout's house' on which to build a hotel. The ground they purchased was actually, in earlier times, Kelday's Court and house. The contractor was John M. Aitken and the foundation stone was laid on 23rd June, 1886, with full Masonic honours. In August 1887, the hotel was open for business.

141. An illustration indicating that the Grand Hotel was now open. August 1887

D. & G. Kay took over the building in 1888 and bought it in 1900, along with their brother Theodore. Over the next 50 years a series of managers were appointed until Mrs Jemima Henry bought The Grand from the Kay family in 1950. The next owner was her daughter Irene Cheyney (née Henry), and then James Bewick who was Irene's second husband. In 1980 local businessman Charlie Fordyce became the proprietor and he had elaborate plans for the hotel but these did not materialise. The hotel changed hands again in 1984 when it was bought by Tulloch of Shetland Ltd and Mr and Mrs Neil Wilkins. The following year, Posers Nightclub was opened. The Grand was taken over by the present owners, J. W. Gray Ltd, in late 1993. Renovations were carried out in 1999.

Mrs Bouwmeister, the widow of a Dutch physician, managed a private hotel in the house she rented at 92 Commercial Street (now the north part of J. G. Rae Ltd). In 1849 Lady Franklin, accompanied by her niece, resided here while in Shetland hoping to hear news of her husband Sir John Franklin who was lost on an expedition to the north-west passage in 1845. Lady Franklin was unaware that he had died in 1847.[16]

142. The Royal Hotel centre right (now Boots). c.1900

One hotel that changed hands, and also names, many times, was situated at 173 Commercial Street (Boots). An upper storey to this property belonging to Robert Linklater, draper and hosier, was added in 1868 when it became the Royal Hotel.[17] Mrs Sarah Mattinson was hotel keeper of the Commercial Hotel[18] here until 1871 when William L. B. Tait took over as the Thule Hotel[19] and later became licensee. Mr Tait died in 1874 and his widow, Mrs Ann Tait, continued to manage the hotel. By 1876 it had become the Zetland Hotel, 'enlarged and refurbished', with Alexander Gordon as proprietor.[20] The hotel changed hands again in 1880 with Aberdonian William Cowie taking charge of what he called Cowie's Hotel.[21] The following year he reverted the name to the Commercial Hotel and then to the Royal Hotel.[22] By 1886 it was advertised as Cowie's Royal Hotel.[23]

During the 1880s, John Byrne, an Irishman, occupied the house above 1 Charlotte Place (currently the Save the Children shop) which had previously been Mr P. E. Petrie's private hotel. Mr Byrne called his establishment Byrne's Temperance Hotel. However, when he left in 1888 to cross the street to become manager of the Royal Hotel, his former hotel building was let to Mr Greig, hairdresser.[24] About 1905 the Royal ceased to be a hotel and became simply the Royal Bar,[25] but operated as a restaurant during prohibition in the 1920s. In 1930 Lipton's opened a branch in the Royal Buildings[26] and thereafter commenced a series of small supermarkets, the last being Presto. The present occupier is Boots.

Mr Byrne's employment at the Royal Hotel was short-lived as in 1890 he opened the Albert Hotel, in Albert Court (which is towards the rear of The Lounge Bar, between Pirate Lane and Law Lane). The same year he opened the Albert Café in the Coffee House at the top of Garthspool Road[27] (presently the site of Allied Taxis). After Mr Byrne died in 1907, the Albert Hotel ceased to operate and the building reverted to a dwelling house.

As an increasing numbers of travellers made their way to Shetland the standard of accommodation in boarding houses, inns and hotels improved.

Despite all the changes in Lerwick over the years the Queens Hotel and The Grand are still in operation.

143. Byrne's Temperance Hotel. c.1886

Smugglers' Tunnels, or Cellars?

144.

Fred Irvine (1890-1976), a painter and decorator to trade, was also a well-known and respected artist. He lived at the south end of Commercial Street in The Knowe, where he also had his studio. In 1952 he published a small booklet in which, through his drawings, he illustrated historical events and stories and left the reader to decide whether or not he/she believed them to be factual. Some of the information was accurate, while some was less so. However, the references to smugglers' tunnels have proved to have some substance. He proposed that the old town of Lerwick was built by smugglers, namely the merchants, and indicated the sites of numerous smugglers' caves or tunnels.[1]

In a reprint he asserted that, as the merchants' houses of old Lerwick were built on the seashore with their back doors opening towards the harbour, contraband cargo could be landed without much fear of interruption from revenue officers. Most of these houses had very ingenious places to conceal smuggled goods. Buildings on the opposite side of the street had this disadvantage compensated by means of a subterranean passage leading from the house or garden under the street to emerge at the seashore at some skilfully disguised entrance.[2]

145. *The entrance to the tunnel or cave was situated here in the garden at the rear of the derelict Stout's House. Nice Court (now Hayfield Court) is on the left and 2-8 Commercial Street is shown upper right. 1962*

The extent of smuggling is highlighted by the fact that in 1798 so much illegal gin had been bought by the merchants during the previous two years that there was a shortage of money in the islands.[3]

Stories have been handed down that suggest the south end of Commercial Street was a particularly notorious area for smuggling. Naturally, due to the covert practice of smuggling, locations were not documented at the time it took place.

Original smugglers' tunnels have been identified as far as possible along with cellars, or parts of a tunnel converted for use as a cellar, associated with the shops along Commercial Street.

It was said that the entrance to a smuggler's tunnel existed under the wooden pier at Murray's Lodberry (not to be confused with the lodberry at the Queens Hotel), which is the site of the present Lerwick Boating Club.[4] In earlier times the area had been a renowned spot for smuggling contraband cargo. In the 1860s the lodberry was occupied by Sinclair and Hardie, joiners, and their workshop had been built on top of an old store. Apparently, when part of the premises had been previously altered, subterranean passages about four feet (1.25m) in height were discovered and were said to lead to green fields.[5] This could well have been the case because older Lerwegians remember, when they were young, using as a gang hut a "whalebone covered cave" at the back of the old, derelict Stout's House.[6] It was remembered that young boys were seen running down from St Magnus Scottish Episcopal Church Sunday school "to play in the smugglers' cave".[7] In the 1960s, prior to the demolition of the old buildings to provide a site for the new Stout's Court housing scheme, the cave was identifiable by a large opening in the ground.[8]

Incidentally, according to the grandson of a former resident of Greenrig House, a smugglers' tunnel led from the house to the seashore.[9] A previous owner had no knowledge of this tale and the present owner has found no evidence of such a tunnel. However, he did receive complaints from neighbours regarding alleged loud music being played. Subsequent investigation revealed the source of the noise to originate from the previously mentioned Lerwick Boating Club premises.[10] Could it have been

146. *Looking south along Commercial Street, from left, is Jim Inkster's garage, The Sea Door, the space is now filled by Lerwick Boating Club, then 12 Commercial Street, and on the right protruding into the street is 17 Commercial Street (or Da Roost Hoose). 1950s*

that the music had travelled from the club through the old tunnel via Stout's Court to the house?

A tunnel did exist from the cellar of MacBeath's House, now the Sea Door, under Commercial Street and Ross Court opposite. The walls of the tunnel were built of stone and lime with a whale-bone roof and clay floor and it exited through an old well in the Court's garden.[11] In the 1960s, shortly before Ross Court was demolished, the tunnel could only be partially accessed as the middle contained rubble almost to the roof.[12] As a consequence of increased traffic it was subsequently filled in for safety reasons.

The buildings at Ross Court are very old, dating back to at least 1670.[13] It was named after William Ross, or 'Bombardier Ross', who came to Lerwick about 1781 and settled. His son John had a shop in the Court where the family lived.[14] The adjoining building built in 1653 is mentioned in 1670 as William

147. *Looking north along Commercial Street in the 1950s. On the left is the garden wall at Nice Court (now Hayfield Court), then the Meeting House, and Ross Court which was situated opposite The Sea Door, then 27-29 Commercial Street. 1950s*

148. The entrance to Raven's Court is in the centre. Early 1960s

149. The entrance to the tunnel at Seafield Court. 2010

Tyrie's House, and then as the Meeting House in 1733. It was divided into flats by the 1750s and James Vance had a school on the upper floor in 1756.[15]

It was suggested that an old smugglers' cave ran from a lodberry under South Commercial Street to emerge though the kitchen cupboard of a dwelling in Raven's Court.[16] A former resident of the house which was situated at the entrance to the Court, confirmed the presence of a passage with an entrance in his kitchen.[17] When the house was demolished in the 1960s a hole in the ground was found, big enough for a man to hide in (most likely from the Press Gang).[18] However, in a house in the Court, which adjoined Irvinesgord, there was a trap door in the kitchen with wooden steps that led down to a tunnel from where the sound of the sea could be heard.[19] None of these houses now exist and no entrance to any tunnel has been found in or near The Lodberrie.

One tunnel actually still does exist. It runs from a house in Seafield Court, under Chromate Lane, then along and under the back of the buildings in a southward direction. It has been said that the exit is somewhere in the courtyard of Lochend House, but it has never been found. The entrance is in Seafield Court and the tunnel has stone-built walls and a flagged ceiling, and like the others it is about four feet (1.25m) high.[20] It is currently used as a store. A member of the family who once ventured into the tunnel travelled through it for some distance and estimated that he had reached the

150. *Location of Murray's Hol. c.1880*

vicinity of Lochend House before turning back "as the air got too bad and there were dead rats". The part of the tunnel that is inside the house was blocked up several years ago when a new kitchen was created.[21]

To the south of Hay's Lodberry was the location of Murray's Hol, a well-known and favourite place for depositing and spiriting away smuggled tobacco, gin, cigars, etc. in the 1700s. This was a passage from the sea with an arched roof from which a subterranean passage ran under the present Queens Hotel, and Commercial Street, to emerge in a garden at the top of Scottshall Court.[22] John Murray, who married Elizabeth Scott in 1781, owned the Court.[23] In later years Murray's Hol was used for the more mundane purpose of buying and storing whelks![24]

151. *Underground passage discovered in 1967 during the construction of Church Road. Joe Gray, roads engineer, hands over a find*

152. Fred Irvine's illustration shows what is now the Royal Bank of Scotland on the left, and P. L. Angus, The Shetland Bookshop, on the right (now demolished). 1952

In 1952 a lorry was reversing close alongside the front of the Queens Hotel when the street collapsed and the rear wheels came to rest on the sill of a window. When the lorry was removed the large opening in the street revealed a ten foot (approximately 3m) drop and massive whalebone lintels, in a deteriorating state, which formed the roof of the tunnel for a distance of 40 feet (13m) from the north corner of the hotel to its door. Part of it had at one time been blocked up and converted for use as a coal cellar. The hole was then completely filled in.[25]

In 1967, during the construction of Church Road, a tunnel or cellar came to light. The photograph shows Joe Gray, roads engineer, in the hole handing over what most certainly looks like a half bottle. What was discovered may have been part of the cellar of Seaview Stores, grocer, provision & wine merchant, which had just been demolished. The shop was situated to the right of the hole.[26]

According to Fred Irvine, a smugglers' cave was discovered when workmen were making alterations to the Commercial Bank (now Royal Bank of Scotland). It contained empty cases and some casks, one of which contained wine.[27] A local man vividly recalled that around about 1932 he ran down to Commercial Street from school after hearing a rumour that a smugglers' tunnel had been found. It was located at the northwest side of the bank (the opposite side from Queens Lane), and the roof consisted of whalebones, some of which were broken.[28]

In December 1932, an underground cellar or tunnel was discovered, probably the same as previously mentioned, at the foot of the garden behind the Commercial Bank during the demolition of an old building to allow extensive alterations to the bank premises. Workmen said it was about 10 feet (3.05m) below the level of the ground. Soil had been built on top of its roof to form a wide terrace at the foot of the sloping garden. It was substantially built of stone and lime, was 14 feet (4.25m) long, six feet (1.83m) wide and 6-7 feet (1.83-2.15m) high. The roof consisted of two layers of stout sections of whales' ribs laid across the top from wall to wall. Most of them were soft and crumbly having deteriorated with age, but others were hard and tough and could only be broken with considerable difficulty. Some of these bones were six to nine inches (15-23cm) in breadth and several inches thick, and on top were several inches of soft blue-grey clay resembling putty in consistency, possibly to keep the passage dry. Above the whale bone ceiling were stone slabs 1 ½ inches (4cm) thick and the passage had a door at one corner.[29]

It is interesting that the bank was built on the site of an earlier building in which James Ross Spence set up in business as a merchant, shipping agent and broker in 1839. He knew all the Dutch skippers who came to Lerwick and his shop displayed Dutch clogs in its window. It would seem logical to think that he was in the very best position to be involved in smuggling activities and in particular from the fact that, in 1843, he succeeded his deceased father Balfour as Dutch consul.[30] Balfour Spence was a merchant and Lloyd's agent who had been involved in smuggling on an agency basis through a London firm whose ships carried legal cargoes but also contraband.[31]

On several occasions when excavations were taking place near and below Commercial Street, whale bone roofs were discovered over rough recesses which were believed to have been smugglers' caves at one time.

Further along Commercial Street, what was described as a 'smuggler's hole' was discovered in October 1904 when the north part of the building presently occupied by Conochies, at 74-78 Commercial Street, was set back to widen the street. This area was known as the Roost. The hole extended a good distance along the street and legend has it that in the mists of time it was possible to reach the Hillhead through this subterranean passage, but this has never been verified.[32]

However, a former resident of Pitt Lane remembers, in the 1950s, unexpectedly finding an underground passage in his garden. While digging a hole to set tatties his stepfather suddenly disappeared to shoulder level down an opening, which transpired to be a well-constructed stone passage that ran under the lane towards what is now the car park between Quendale Lane and Hill Lane. He also recalled that in the early 1970s, when a JCB was preparing the site for the swimming pool (now the car park), without warning it sank into a similar passage.[33] Was the legend actually based on fact? We may never know.

In 1905 a passage, possibly for storing smuggled goods, was discovered when a site was being provided for Mr E. S. Reid Tait's building, now housing at street level Ninian at 80 and Aurora Jewellery at 82 Commercial Street, and at the rear Coffee & Keetchin and Lerwick DIY at

153. *The steps at Angus's Closs near Harrison Square, between Lerwick DIY and the Cancer Research charity shop, photographed in 2011. A tunnel was found adjacent to the steps in 1904*

80-82 Harrison Square. The tunnel was said to extend from the steps at Angus' Closs (between Aurora Jewellery and Fat Little Pony), round to the front of the shop occupied by Gilbert Angus, presently Fat Little Pony at 84 Commercial Street.[34]

In 1998, when Commercial Street was being repaved and old sewer/water pipes were replaced, a blocked up tunnel measuring about four feet in height with a curved stone roof was rediscovered outside Da Noost at 86 Commercial Street. The owner had been aware of this tunnel, extending from the cellar, when he bought the property but had never been in it. It ran under Commercial Street in the direction of R. W. Bayes at 143 and contained some empty bottles, presumably left by the shop's previous owner, W. A. Robertson & Sons, licensed grocers and provision merchant. The cellar was filled in at that time.[35]

A written account about smuggling involved the Kelday family. Kelday's Court was situated where the Grand Hotel now stands. The court was enclosed by a stone wall and it was said that the gateway, with its stone vases on the side posts, was more like the approach to a country mansion than an entry to a town house. The house stood with its front to the south, with a large garden to the west. In the gable facing Commercial Street was a shop. The building was the residence of James Kelday who, in the 18th century, was a well-known Lerwick merchant along with his brother John. James became known as "the man who cheated the smuggler". The story goes that a tunnel led up from the foreshore to a cellar underneath the house. One night, by some prearrangement, the skipper of a foreign ship landed several barrels of liquor and rolled them up the underground passage into Kelday's cellar. Leaving them there he returned to his vessel to wait for daylight, when he would settle his account with the merchant. In the meantime Mrs Kelday, apparently being aware of the storing

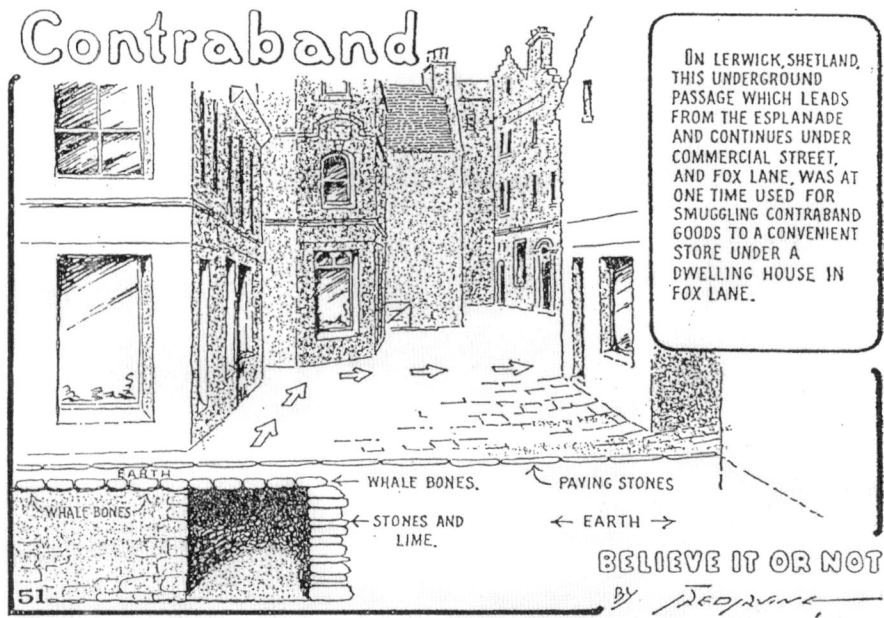

154. *Fred Irvine's illustration showing suggested tunnel in front of M&Co, leading to Fox Lane. 1952*

of the barrels, instructed some men to remove them to another location. When the skipper appeared and asked to have his bill paid, James Kelday was able to plead entire ignorance of the business and to show the indignant skipper an empty cellar. A public dispute about smuggled drink would not have been appropriate but, in an act of retaliation, when the merchant opened his front door next day he found miniature gallows erected outside with an effigy of him hanging from it.[36]

It is highly possible that the underground passage leading to Kelday's cellar was part of the one discovered in 1932 during roadworks for the installation of electricity cables. It extended along the front of what is now the north part of J. G. Rae Ltd at 92 Commercial Street. A broad passage reached towards Robert Ollason's shop at 155 Commercial Street (now the Stage Door), where two deep vaults were found. It was evident that the passage had at one time connected with the top part of Greig's Closs, which led from the Esplanade to Commercial Street, but the Closs had been blocked up when the building had been restructured at some point.[37] However, it was not until 1955, when the stone flags were removed to resolve a water leakage, that workmen rediscovered the passage and it was filled in.[38]

Employees of nearby Stove & Smith at 98 Commercial Street remember its cellar under the street. They described that at the far end there was an opening into a narrow tunnel in the direction of Fox Lane which had been blocked up at some point by a wall, leaving only a small gap at the top, too small to get through. This may well have been a smugglers' tunnel. It was said that an individual going down the adjoining Nicolson's Closs unexpectedly fell down a hole which subsequently became Stove and Smith's coal cellar.[39] A manhole cover can still be seen in the Closs.

Fred Irvine's illustration, entitled 'Contraband', indicates that a passage existed under Commercial Street in front of what is now M&Co.[40] From 1938 until 1976 the shop was occupied by the Scottish Co-op Society Ltd. In 1976 Greenwald's shop opposite was due for demolition and concern was expressed that the resulting heavy traffic involved in removing debris could result in the collapse of the passage. Dennis Coutts' photograph, taken in March 1976, shows the manager of the Co-op, Jim Ganson, in the cellar, or passage, that had been used to store soap. The old steps behind Mr Ganson originally led up to Commercial Street but, at the time the photograph was taken, simply ended with a small grille from where it was possible to see people walking along the street. The cellar was filled in shortly after the photograph was taken. Due to the presence of these steps, and the size of the cellar, it is unlikely that this was a smugglers' tunnel. (Incidentally, the Co-op relocated to new premises at North Road, now Frank Williamson, that same year.)

Originally, in front of Harry's on Commercial Street there were steps leading down to shop basements. This area was covered over in the early 1900s when the street was widened[41] and glass panels were inserted to light the passage below. These can be seen in the pavement. However, at the far end there is a short passage leading to what appears to be an old, dark and unwelcoming cellar or part of a tunnel – an ideal location to hide illicit booty.[42]

In 1998, during the repaving project, expectation was high that further forgotten tunnels would be discovered but this was not the case. Apart from the old cellar discovered outside Da Noost, the only other structure unearthed was an ancient sea wall near Faerdie-Maet, formerly Solotti's, at 42 Commercial Street.[43]

This information has been collated to record an important part of Lerwick's history and a somewhat romantic activity carried out mainly in the 18th and 19th centuries. Many of the passages may well have been utilised as shop cellars but those that were described as having whalebone roofs were most probably smugglers' tunnels.

155. *The manager of the Co-op, Jim Ganson, in underground passage in front of the shop on 27th March, 1976*

Christmas Shopping in the 1950s

In the 1950s money was scarce, but buying Christmas presents was a pleasure that most people enjoyed. Apart from birthdays it was often the only other time that gifts were received.

A small number of cards were sent to relatives and close friends and each was individually purchased and chosen with the illustration and verse suitable for the recipient.

Most shops and businesses had calendars which were issued to their loyal customers; the version with a pocket to hold all manner of paper throughout the year, such as bills and receipts, were sought after. Some grocer shops gave customers a tea caddy.

Christmas trees arrived by the 'North of Scotland steamer' at Victoria Pier, usually about a week before Christmas, and there was great excitement in households around the town when the delivery truck appeared.

Popular presents exchanged were tins of biscuits or loose tea – both useful. Visits were made to grocer shops along Commercial Street such as Lipton Ltd (now Boots); Scottish Co-op Society Ltd (now M&Co); D. & G. Kay (now Begg Shoes & Bags); W. A. Robertson (now Da Noost); R. & C. Robertson (now The Camera Centre); T. J. Anderson (now Tourist Office); and Seaview Stores (demolished when Church Road was constructed).

In addition to toys, many bairns could expect to find an orange, an apple, a peerie tin of sweeties and a sugary pig in their sock or pillow case on Christmas morning, and several fruit and confectionery shops sold all these. Namely P. Solotti & Son Ltd (now Faerdie-Maet); Ellesmere Stores (now part of D. & G. Leslie); Peter Leisk & Co (now High Level Music Centre); The Flower Shop on the north side of Bank Lane; Jas. Manson opposite the Grand Hotel; and Alex. Manson at the foot of Burns Lane (now Mirrie Dancers Chocolatier). Another popular shop was, and is, Universal Stores, still

156. Mrs Elizabeth J. Yates' Christmas advertisement

referred to by many as 'Sweetie Lowrie's' after the original proprietor, Laurence W. Smith. In the 1950s, Universal Stores received supplies of Kunzle Cakes every week. These were small fancies with a sponge mixture in a chocolate case, rather than the normal pastry, covered with flavoured butter cream and topped with an almond or sugar-coated fruit sweet.

Many folk will fondly remember as a child the excitement of going upstairs in Stove & Smith (Scottish Hydro Electric until 2016) to meet Santa and pick a gift from the bran tub – a barrel filled with sawdust in which all the little wrapped items, such as a toy of some description or colouring pencils, had been placed. Considered time was taken in making a choice as each unseen parcel had to be found and then felt all over in an attempt to identify its content and therefore acquire the desired present. Stove & Smith was an ironmongers and hardware merchant with tools, paints, ropes, seeds and plants, agricultural implements and fishing tackle, among other necessities, available on the ground floor while upstairs was a treasure trove with china, fancy goods, toys and games.

A similar shop was R. Goudie & Son (now The Wine Shop) which sold Airfix model kits. Opposite Goudie's was E. J. Yates, commonly referred to as Keetie Bruce's (now Da Fish Bowl). It stocked china, crystal, glass, cutlery, fancy goods and toys of every description and was

157. *The entrance to Mrs Elizabeth J. Yates' shop*

158. *R. Goudie & Son*

159. *Alex. Manson, H. & J. Greenwald, and James S. Smith, butcher*

the dealer for Meccano, Hornby Train and Dinky toys. Everyone over a certain age remembers the window displays here and this shop was another popular venue for meeting Santa.

W. K. Conochie Ltd, as now, sold newspapers, stationery, books and office items but, in addition, stocked radios, fishing tackle, golfing, and tennis equipment.

Robert Ollason, bookseller, stationer, newsagent and fancy goods merchant (now The Stage Door) also stocked toys and games.

Brush sets, manicure sets, powder compacts, cigarette lighters and cases, shaving sets, razors, wallets, rings, jewellery, watches, clocks and pens were available from The Gift Shop owned by Mrs Queenie McWhirter (now the north part of J. G. Rae Ltd).

Jewellery and watches could also be obtained from Harry Greenwald (Klaize until 2017), in addition to a wide assortment of clothing.

The current N-graved and Shetland Parliamentary Office at 169 and 171 Commercial Street respectively, were photographer Eddie Sinclair's shop, which had an extensive stock of special gifts, jewellery and silverware.

Charles B. Stout, chemist and pharmacist (proprietor W. D. C. Binns), at the Medical Hall (now Loose Ends) sold 'beauty preparations' and cosmetics, as did A. L. Laing at the Market Cross, also A. A. Porteous (now the part of the Bank of Scotland next to Hangcliff Lane). The proprietor, Alex. Campbell, better known as 'Spew', was a colourful character and will be remembered by many for his musical ability and eccentricity.

A trip to da Street was not complete without purchasing bread and meat. Malcolmson & Co (presently Aa' Fired Up) was the only bakeshop but M. & R. Georgeson, whose bakery was at 9 Clairmont Place, had a shop at 84 Commercial Street (now Fat Little Pony).

There were several butcher shops. James S. Smith at the foot of Charlotte Street (Continental Tastes until October 2017); Scottish Co-op Society Ltd (the part of M&Co nearest Scottish Hydro Electric for some years); and A. W. Herd (now the part of Conochie's adjacent to lower Reform Lane). Anyone who ever ate a deep-fat fried Herd's pie will never forget the experience – totally unhealthy, but delicious! Other butcher shops were Lerwick Meat Co (now Red Cross shop); W. (Wills) R. Jamieson (now the part of A. L. Laing's nearest the Tourist Office); Smith & Co (now Vaila Fine Art); and Peterson & Co (Patter's), on the south side of Chromate Lane.

Tired and hungry shoppers could visit P. Solotti & Son; Halcrow's Restaurant (above Tatties & Point and the Red Cross shop); or the Old Rock Cafe (in the premises between Save the Children and Harry's).

Another popular eating place, situated above Peter Leisk's shop and run by Albert Stevenson, was the Victoria Restaurant (now part of High Level Music Centre). Fish and chips, fried by Albert, were also available on ground level from a hatch opening on to the Market Cross. There was nearly always a queue of folk waiting to be served by Joan Jamieson, 'Peerie Joanne' or Juno.

The younger generation flocked to Lillian & Frank Chadwick's Hygienic Snack Bar at 59 Commercial Street, opposite the Queens Hotel, to listen to the latest hits on the jukebox, the first to arrive in Shetland in 1953.

Although shops on Commercial Street have changed over the years, the following sentiment expressed in a card from the 1950s still remains appropriate today:

"*May past and present both unite
To make your Christmas calm and bright,
With memories blest, and hope to cheer
Throughout a good and gladsome Year!*"

160. *A. W. Herd, butcher and M. & R. Georgeson, baker and confectioner. Late 1950s*

161. *Peter Leisk & Co on the left. The door in the centre led upstairs to the Victoria Restaurant and the window on the far right was where fish and chips were sold from a hatch*

Hame Wi Dee Lowrie

Over the years there have been numerous songs written in dialect, some set to original music and some to well-known tunes. Most are humorous and tell the story of a real life occurrence and were sung, and still are, at concerts throughout Shetland.

One such song is *Hame wi dee Lowrie* and, although the first chorus is familiar to many, the complete verses may not be remembered. It is probable that David Hunter Sandison of Catfirth, South Nesting, composed it in the 1930s. He was born in 1893 and died in 1956. In the song Lowrie refers to places in Nesting before he goes to Lerwick for Up-Helly-A'.

I winder what's happened ta Osla,
I winder what ails 'er wi me?
For every time noo at I meet 'er,
Shö roars oot as lood as can be:
"Geng hame wi dee, hame wi dee Lowrie,
Ta come efter me du's no blate;
For I want a lad at is bonny,
No een wi a face laek a skate."

I göd in alang 'er ee Försday
Ta see if shö'd come for a slud*
Trow da gairdens o Gerts an ta Finstoons,
An mebbe as far as da Dudds:
"Geng hame wi dee, hame wi dee Lowrie!"
Shö roared as I göd for 'er door,
"Dey'd be föls at wid geng ta da Finnstoons,
Ta stick ida aert-bogs an smore."

Shö came ta da hall here ee Tiesday,
Whin da rod-hogs wis haein der dance;
Ta win hame wi 'er ida moarnin,
Tocht I what a whaal o a shance:
"Geng hame wi dee, hame wi dee Lowrie!"
Shö roared as 'er airm he took;
Shö was mittened wi Rasmie fae Catfirth,
An hame dey baith göd ta Essook.

I axed 'er ta come in ta Lerook
On da nicht hit was Up-Helly-A',
An whan at da Dreel Hall I met 'er,
Shö stöd up an sang afore aa:
"Geng hame wi dee, hame wi dee Lowrie!
Du shörly tinks I man be glig,
Du's been oot da Nort Rodd at Frankie's –
Dee braeth is jöst laek a rum kig."

I bocht 'er black sugar fae Lipton's,
A bottle o hair oil fae aald Leys,
A pair o red gertans fae Eunson's,
An fae Reid Tait's a pair o new stays:
"Geng hame wi dee, hame wi dee Lowrie,
I nedder want dee or dee gifts:
Red gertans an stays I never wear dem,
Black sugar gies me da brunt rift."

"Noo Osla if du's sittin listenin,
Du kens as I'm telling nae lees,
Jöst tak dis nicht for a lesson –
I'm comin nae mair eftir dee.
Geng hame wi dee, hame wi dee Osla,
Is du awaar what du's done is a shame?
I'm faan in wi a braa ting fae Gletness,
I'm awa noo ta see me lass hame."

Although the Lerwick shops mentioned in the song no longer exist their names are immortalised in the verses. The buildings remain though, and here is some brief information about these and the occupants.

The first place that Lowrie visited was the 'Dreel Hall'. The building was erected in 1904 as HQ, drill hall and gymnasium for the 7th Volunteer Battalion The Gordon Highlanders. It was requisitioned during the Second World War as HQ for the Shetland Defence Battalion and in December 1942 the Drill Hall officially became the Garrison Theatre and was used to entertain the troops.

The Dreel Hall was first used for Up-Helly-A' in 1910 and continued as a venue until 1939, with a break during the years of the First World War. It was where country folk enjoyed the festival.

In the song, Osla accused Lowrie of having been "oot da Nort Rodd at Frankie's". During the years of prohibition, from 1920 until 1947, Lerwick was dry. F. J. Sandison was a licensed wholesaler supplying beer, spirits and wine and these could be legally bought in bulk. Another option was 'under the counter' transactions and Frankie's had the reputation of being a notorious shebeen. Lowrie had obviously called along for a dram. The building is now a private residence.

162. *The Dreel Hall, now the Garrison Theatre. 1904*

Lowrie then purchased some black sugar from Liptons Ltd. The shop opened in 1930 at 173 Commercial Street, previously The Royal Bar. Liptons changed to Templetons in the 1970s, followed by Prestos and then Safeways. The premises is now occupied by Boots UK Ltd. Osla complained that the sugar he had bought would give her severe indigestion!

The hair oil from Leys wasn't appreciated either. Alexander A. Leys, hairdresser, was situated at 133 Commercial Street at the foot of Reform Lane, opposite the present day Ninian. In 1916 he had taken over John S. Lillie's hairdresser shop and Mr Leys worked there until 1944, when Thomas Russell acquired the business.

The red gertans or garters were brought from William Eunson, draper, who started trading in 1929 from his shop in Harbour Street, for some time Rod & Line Fishing Tackle, then the Shetland Jazz Club Bop Shop. Readers may remember Charlie Moar there. In 1934 Mr Eunson moved up around the corner to the premises on Market

163. *The North Road. Burgess Street is on the left, then 'Frankie's' (Frank Sandison's shop) and Pig Street on the right. 1904*

164. *Lipton's, 173 Commercial Street. 1938*

Street that previously had been occupied by the Turk's Head Public Bar (now part of Market House). In 1939 he built new premises at 22-24 North Road, now Shetland Charitable Trust.

Lowrie bought Osla stays from Reid Tait's. Stays was another name for an old fashioned stiff corset. Edwin Seymour (E. S.) Reid Tait had premises built on Commercial Street in 1905. Ladies clothing was sold at No. 80 while the men's department was at No. 82. In 1943 the Scottish Co-operative Wholesale Society Ltd bought the property. The shops are now occupied by Ninian and Aurora respectively.

Perhaps the trials and tribulations of a modern day Lowrie at Up-Helly-A' may result in a new song being composed.

* To slip away during a break between showers

165. *Ley's Hairdresser, 133 Commercial Street. Directly opposite was E. S. Reid Tait's draper shop. 1938*

REFERENCES

The Dutch Connection
1. Boelmans Kranenburg, H. A. H., *The Netherland Fisheries and the Shetland Islands* in *Shetland & the Outside World 1469-1969* (Oxford 1983) p. 98
2. Smith Hance D., *Shetland Life and Trade 1550-1914* (Edinburgh 1984) p. 328
3. *ibid.*, p. 342
4. Irvine James W., *Lerwick the birth and growth of an island town* (Lerwick 1985) p. 16
5. Smith Hance D., *Shetland Life and Trade 1550-1914* (Edinburgh 1984) p. 27
6. Coull James R., *The Third Statistical Account of Scotland Vol. XXB The County of Shetland* (Edinburgh 1985) p. 57
7. Low Geo3 J., *Hollanders in Shetland* (Lerwick 1973)
8. It has also been suggested by other fishermen that this took place on arrival
9. Correspondence received from Gus van der Loodt regarding Grootjes Poortje August 16 2007
10. *ii Shetland* July 2012 Issue 67 p. 56
11. www.vissersnamenmonumentscheveningen.nl

The Coffee House
1. Robertson Margaret Stuart, *Sons and Daughters of Shetland 1800-1900* (Lerwick 1991) p. 112
2. SA Valuation Roll Lerwick Landward 1885-86
3. *The Shetland Times* July 12 1890
4. SA Valuation Roll Lerwick Landward 1893-94
5. *ibid.*, 1894-98
6. Crawford James M., *The Parish of Lerwick, 1701-1901* (Lerwick 1901) pp. 90-91
7. SA, D.1/133 pp. 96-98 Part of *De Spiegel*, Amsterdam 15 December 1906, with article 'Among the fishermen in Lerwick'
8. *The Shetland Times* May 20 1911
9. SA Valuation Rolls Lerwick Landward 1912-13, 1913-14, 1914-15

The 'Fever' Hospital
1. Unfortunately, to date, no record has been found
2. Kulen Johannes van, *Kaart van de rede van Lerwick in de Shetland Eilanden*, 1725-1755, Amsterdam
3. Brand Rev. John, *A brief description of Orkney, Zetland, Pightland-firth and Caithness* (Edinburgh 1883) pp. 127-128
4. *ibid.*, p. 109
5. Edmondston Arthur, *View of the ancient and present state of the Zetland Islands, Vol. II* (Edinburgh 1809) pp. 85-88
6. Sandison William, *A Shetland Merchant's Day-Book in 1762* (Lerwick 1934) p. 6
7. Edmondston Arthur, *View of the ancient and present state of the Zetland Islands, Vol. II* (Edinburgh 1809) pp. 87-88
8. Cowie Robert, *Shetland and its inhabitants* (Aberdeen 1871) p. 60

9. Leaflet from The Jenner Museum, Berkley, Gloucestershire ND
10. *John o' Groat Journal* 19 January 1863 p. 2
11. Irvine James W., *Lerwick the birth and growth of an island town* (Lerwick 1985) pp. 80-81
12. Minute of the Commissioners of Police, 25 June 1841 p. 209
13. Minute of meeting of Trustees for the Heritors of Lerwick, 28 December 1841 p. 12
14. Minute of certain Trustees for the Heritors of Lerwick, 28 August 1845 pp. 51-52
15. SA SC12/6/1851/44
16. Flinn Derek, *Travellers in a bygone Shetland: An Anthology* (Edinburgh 1989) p. 231
17. Tait E. S. Reid, *A Lerwick Miscellany* (Lerwick 1955) p. 58
18. Excerpts from the minutes of meetings of the Feuars and Heritors of Lerwick (Lerwick 1909) 28 May 1872 p. 9
19. SA D25/86 Report by Alexander Stewart, Chief Officer of Police and Sanitary Inspector for the Burgh of Lerwick 21 November 1873
20. SA CO 6/21/1 Minutes of Combination Hospital, 1885-1926
21. *The Shetland Times* 25 March 1905 p. 5
22. Medical Officer of Health and Sanitary Inspector reports for County of Zetland, Mainland District for year ending 31 December 1929 p. 22
23. www.cdc.gov/smallpox/history/history.htm

Twageos and Twageos House
1. *The Shetland Times* September 13 1902
2. Census for Lerwick 1871
3. Oral information from Thomas Goudie 1999
4. *ibid.*
5. *The Shetland Times* June 1 1935
6. Conversation with Brian Smith, Archivist 2015
7. SA GD150/2575A/1 James Isaacson's chamberlain's accounts with the Earl of Morton
8. *The New Shetlander* Hairst Number 70 1964
9. Sutherland Paul J., *Morton Lodge No. 89, 250 years of a Lerwick Institution 1762-2012* (Lerwick 2012) p. 10
10. *The Shetland Times* September 13 1902
11. SA 4/523/1 December 18 1827
12. Sutherland Paul J., *Morton Lodge No. 89, 250 years of a Lerwick Institution 1762-2012* (Lerwick 2012) p. 11
13. Crawford James M., *The Parish of Lerwick 1701-1901* (Lerwick 1901) p. 40
14. Census for Lerwick 1861-1901
15. *The New Shetlander* Voar Number 179 1992
16. *The New Shetlander* Hairst Number 70 1964
17. *The New Shetlander* Yule Number 71 1964
18. *The New Shetlander* Voar Number 72 1965
19. Irvine James W., *The Dunrossness Story* (Brae 1987) p. 199
20. SA 4/523/9 December 26 1935
21. *The Shetland Times* March 17 1950
22. Personal experience when visiting friend John Rognvaldson in 1950s

23. SA TO/11/89 Letter from Asst. Chief Valuer, Scotland to Ministry of Works Feb. 1958
24. *ibid.*, Letter from Ministry of Works to Lerwick Town Clerk March 1959
25. Oral information from Willie Leask

Gressy Loan and surrounding area
1. Oral information from James Winchester and Emily Knight
2. *The Shetland Times* June 1 1962
3. Oral information from Alice Nicolson and James Winchester 2008
4. *The Shetland Times* May 1945
5. Oral information from James Winchester
6. *The Shetland Times* March 12 1948
7. Irvine James W., *Lerwick the birth and growth of an island town* (Lerwick 1985) p. 216
8. Oral information from Willie Henderson 2014
9. The author's personal knowledge.
10. SA Lerwick Town Council minutes March 1970

Relics of Wartime
1. *Centenary of the Anderson Educational Institute Lerwick 1862-1962* (Lerwick 1962) p. 32
2. Graham John J., *A vehement thirst after knowledge* (Lerwick 1998) p. 197
3. Anderson High School Newsletter Celebrating 150 years issue No.40
4. *Centenary of the Anderson Educational Institute Lerwick 1862-1962* (Lerwick 1962) p. 29
5. Oral information from James Winchester 2008
6. SA Lerwick Town Council minutes March 1970
7. Oral information from George Johnson 2008
8. *Centenary of the Anderson Educational Institute Lerwick 1862-1962* (Lerwick 1962) p. 28
9. Oral information from James Winchester 2008
10. *The Shetland News* October 16 *1947*
11. Lamont Daniel, *Sea-Girt Citadel* (Lerwick 1973) pp. 93-94
12. *The Shetland Times* March 12 1947 p. 8
13. *Shetland Life* December 1980 pp. 8-9
14. *The Shetland Times* December 29 1906

The Hostels – An early history
1. Graham John J., *A vehement thirst after knowledge* (Lerwick 1998) p. 192
2. Robertson, Margaret Stuart, *Sons and Daughters of Shetland 1800-1900* (Lerwick 1991) p. 19
3. *The Shetland Times* August 11 1923
4. Lamont Daniel, *Sea-Girt Citadel* (Lerwick 1973) pp. 93-94
5. http://dictionnaire.sensagent.leparisien.fr/
6. Lamont Daniel, *Sea-Girt Citadel* (Lerwick 1973) p. 94
7. *Centenary of the Anderson Educational Institute Lerwick 1862-1962* (Lerwick 1962) p. 29
8. SA D1/538/3
9. Oral information from Noelle Gordon

10. *The Shetland News* October 9 1947
11. *The Shetland News* October 16 1947
12. *The Shetland News* October 16 1947

The House of Charity
1. *Shetland Life* December 1990
2. *The Shetland Times* June 18 1904
3. *The Shetland Times* January 23 1904
4. SA D11/28/8 *The Scottish Standard Bearers March 1896*, St Magnus Church Lerwick
5. *The Shetland News* January 23 1904
6. *The Shetland Times* January 23 1904
7. *The Shetland Times* June 18 1904
8. Extract from St Magnus Church Registers
9. *The Shetland Times* December 3 1904, Advertisement for Sale of Work
10. *The Shetland Times* June 18 1904
11. *The Shetland Times* July 1 1905
12. *Shetland Life* November 1990
13. *Shetland Life* December 1990
14. *The Shetland News* June 13 1903
15. *The Shetland News* August 26 1920
16. *The Shetland News* March 8 1923
17. SA D54/11/4/2
18. Oral information from Peter Smith. He and Daisy were married there in 1963
19. Oral information from Frances Watt 2013
20. SA D54/11/4/17/1
21. Wallace D.G., *S. Magnus' Episcopal Church Lerwick. A brief history* (Lerwick 1976)

Missions to Seamen Institute (The Flying Angel)
1. Strong L. A. G., *Flying Angel* (London 1956) pp. 18-24
2. *"Da Fishermen's Mission" 1907-2007* (Unst 2007) p. 7
3. *The Shetland News* May 19 1921
4. Nicolson James R., *Lerwick Harbour* (Lerwick 1977) p. 107
5. *The Shetland News* May 19 1921
6. *The Shetland Times* February 26 1921
7. SA Valuation Roll Lerwick 1927-28
8. *The Shetland Times* November 20 1926
9. SA Valuation Roll Lerwick 1927-28
10. Bertie David M., *Scottish Episcopal Clergy 1689-2000* (Edinburgh 2000) p. 529
11. On 4th April 2001 The Missions to Seamen nationally changed its name to 'The Mission to Seafarers'.
12. The Missions to Seamen Lerwick Station, Annual Report 1954
13. *The Shetland Life* October 1993 No. 156 p. 4

Arthur Anderson and Cruising
1. *The Shetland News* August 7 2009
2. *Lerwick Port Authority* Bulletin September 2007

3. City Arts Department-City of Aberdeen *The North Boats* (Aberdeen 1990)
4. Nicolson John, *Arthur Anderson A Founder of the P & O Coy* (Paisley 1914) p. 10
5. Cowsill M. et al., *P & O The Fleet* (Pembrokeshire 1999) p. 3
6. *The Shetland Journal* June 11 1836
7. Howarth D & Howarth S., *The Story of P & O: Peninsular and Oriental Steam Navigation Company (London 1995)* p. 47
8. Nicolson John, *Arthur Anderson A Founder of the P & O Company* (Lerwick 1932) p. 39
9. Howarth D & Howarth S., *The Story of P & O: Peninsular and Oriental Steam Navigation Company* (London 1995) p. 63
10. *ibid.*, pp. 66-67
11. Robertson Margaret Stuart, *Sons and Daughters of Shetland 1800-1900* (Lerwick 1991) p. 3
12. *The New Shetlander* Number 50 April-June 1959
13. *The Shetland Times* August 8 1931
14. Howarth D. & Howarth S., *The Story of P & O: Peninsular and Oriental Steam Navigation Company* (London 1995) pp. 130-135
15. *The Shetland Times* August 8 1931
16. Howarth D. & Howarth S., *The Story of P & O: Peninsular and Oriental Steam Navigation Company* (London 1995) p. 147

The Knowe
1. Oral information from Dennis Coutts 2012
2. Robertson Margaret Stuart, *Sons and Daughters of Shetland 1800-1900* (Lerwick 1991) p. 122
3. Shetland Family History Society
4. Oral information from Dennis Coutts 2012
5. From notes by Margaret Stuart Robertson
6. SA CO/6/7/91 Valuation roll, of the Parish of Lerwick 1859-1860
7. Manson Thomas, *Lerwick during the last Half Century* (Lerwick 1923) p. 212
8. *The Shetland News* January 22 1898
9. Robertson Margaret Stuart, *Sons and Daughters of Shetland 1800-1900* (Lerwick 1991) p. 17
10. SA CO/6/7/109 Assessment roll of the Parish of Lerwick 1888-1889
11. SA SA1/1/19 Census of Shetland – Lerwick 1901
12. SA SC12/6/1928/2 Petition for appointment as executor dative qua. Pursuer: Magnus Frederick Francis Irvine
13. SA AD22/101/1925/2 Report concerning the destruction by fire, of a shop at 22 Commercial Street, occupied by Fred. Irvine, painter & decorator
14. *Mansons' Shetland Almanac 1933*
15. SA *Pictures from Shetland's Past* with newspaper cuttings and typed notes by Reid Tait concerning inaccuracies in Irvine's work 1955-56
16. It is without doubt that frequent visits to The Knowe and long conversations with Fred played a significant part in developing the author's interest and passion for Old Lerwick
17. Oral information from Dennis Coutts

The Old Manse
1. SA1/3/5 1682-92 Register of Sasines
2. Discussion with Margaret Stuart Robertson
3. Sandison William, *A Shetland Merchant's Day-Book in 1762* (Lerwick 1934) pp. 14-15
4. Crawford James M., *The Parish of Lerwick 1701-1901* (Lerwick 1901) p. 21
5. Tait E. S. Reid, *The Hjaltland Miscellany* (Lerwick 1947) p134, footnote 83. "It was William Dick of Wormadale and not William Dick of Fracafield, as erroneously stated in Crawford's 'The Parish of Lerwick, 1701-1901', who sold the house known as the 'Old Manse' to the Heritors of Lerwick to be a Manse to Rev. James Milne, first minister of Lerwick"
6. Crawford James M., *The Parish of Lerwick 1701-1901* (Lerwick 1901) p. 21
7. SA Ballantyne John, Notes of Shetland entries in General Register of Sasines 1617-1780
8. Discussion with Margaret Stuart Robertson
9. Sandison Ronald, *Christopher Sandison, Diarist in an age of Social Change* (Lerwick 1997) p. 145
10. *www.bayanne.info/Shetland/*
11. *Orkney & Shetland Miscellany Vol. 1 Part VI* April 1908 p. 235
12. SA4/523/2 August 21 1865
13. Oral information from Margaret Stuart Robertson
14. *Orkney & Shetland Miscellany Vol. 1 Part VI* April 1908 p. 235
15. SA4/523/6 July 6 1908
16. SA SC12/36/17 p. 361
17. SA4/523/8 December 16 1926
18. SA Valuation Roll Lerwick 1926-1927
19. Wikipedia List of High Commissioners of the United Kingdom to Barbados
20. SA4/523/9 January 4 1936
21. Jamieson Ian, *Shetland's Roll of Honour and Roll of Service 1939-1945* (Lerwick 1990) p. 57
22. SA4/523/11 August 19 1950
23. Wishart Basil, *Memoirs* (Lerwick 1998) p. 85
24. The author's parents, himself and two younger sisters moved from his grandmother's house at Nice Court to the Old Manse
25. *The Shetland News* January 22 1898 *Article Old Lerwick*
26. *New Shetlander* September-October 1949 p. 20
27. Letter from W. N. Sinclair to Lerwick Town Council, dated February 12 1965
28. Oral information from Mary Eunson 2017
29. *The Shetland Times* August 19 2016

Stout's Court
1. Robertson Margaret Stuart, *Sons and Daughters of Shetland 1800-1900* (Lerwick 1991) p. 196
2. SA 833/29.1. 1819
3. SA CS 235 M31/1 Sketch of map 18.12.1795
4. Discussion with Margaret Stuart Robertson

5. Clausen E. J. F. and Manson T. M. Y., *150th Anniversary of Lerwick Parish Church* (Lerwick 1979) p. 3
6. The author's personal knowledge
7. Manson Thomas, *Lerwick during the last Half Century* (Lerwick 1923) pp. 43-44
8. *Mansons' Shetland Almanac Advertiser 1929* p.xxviii
9. Robertson Margaret Stuart, *Sons and Daughters of Shetland 1800-1900* (Lerwick 1991) p. 196
10. *ibid.*, p. 176
11. Tait, E. S. Reid., *A Lerwick Miscellany* (Lerwick 1955) p. 3
12. *The Shetland Times* September 13 1902
13. SA D1/619/8/3 Special Edition of Shetland News. *The Lerwick Paving Case* July 15 1898
14. Robertson M. S., *Sons and Daughters of Shetland 1800-1900* (Lerwick 1991) p. 17
15. Mackay James A., *Islands Postal History Series No. 8 Shetland* (Dumfries 1979) pp. 24-25
16. Irvine James W., *Lerwick the birth and growth of an island town* (Lerwick 1985)
17. Laurenson Graeme A., *Kiwi in the Shetland Scattald* (New Plymouth ND) pp. 100-106
18. The author's personal recollection
19. Irvine James W., *Lerwick the birth and growth of an island town* (Lerwick 1985) p. 244

Kveldsro
1. DSA Architect Biography Report
2. SA4/523/1 January 23 1825
3. Nicolson James R., *Hay & Company Merchants in Shetland* (Lerwick 1982) pp. 8-9
4. *ibid.*, p. 13
5. *ibid.*, p. 22
6. Irvine James W., *Lerwick the birth and growth of an island town* (Lerwick 1985) p. 139
7. Oral information from Stanley Murray 1991
8. 1901 census. The author's Great Grandparents
9. Irvine James W., *Lerwick the birth and growth of an island town* (Lerwick 1985) p. 180
10. Robertson Margaret Stuart, *Sons and Daughters of Shetland 1800-1900* (Lerwick 1991) p. 71
11. *ibid.*, p. 73
12. SA TO Correspondence from J. B. Anderson & Goodlad, Solicitors to Town Clerk 1974
13. Oral information from George Johnson 2014
14. Simpson C., *Da Blinnd Hunder* in *The New Shetlander* Hairst 2006 pp. 38-9
15. Oral information from George Johnson 2014
16. SA TO/11/75 Correspondence from J. B. Anderson & Goodlad, Solicitors to Town Clerk 1974
17. *The Shetland Times* April 19 1991
18. SA SC/12/36/53 p. 481
19. Nicolson, James R., *Lerwick Harbour* (Lerwick 1977) p. 155
20. SA4/523/14 May 17 1966
21. SA TO/11/75 Correspondence from J. B. Anderson & Goodlad, Solicitors to Town Clerk 1974

22. *The Shetland Times* April 11 1969
23. Oral information from Irene Williamson and Jasmine Tulloch 2014
24. *The Shetland Times* June 21 1991
25. Oral information from Marjorie Barrie 2014

Craigie's Court and Quendale House
1. *The Shetland News* January 22 1898 *Article Old Lerwick*
2. Sandison William, *A Shetland Merchant's Day-Book in 1762* (Lerwick 1934) p. 24
3. SA SC12/53/12 Disposition and settlement by Captain John Craigie, March 18 1855
4. Manson Thomas, *Lerwick during the last Half Century* (Lerwick 1923) p. 6
5. Robertson Margaret Stuart, *Sons and Daughters of Shetland 1800-1900* (Lerwick 1991) p. 65
6. Lerwick Census 1901
7. Manson T. M. Y., Council News – No. 16 November 1991 p. 11
8. SA4/523/7 April 11 and May 3 1918
9. SA4/523/10 January 27 1939
10. Irvine James W., *The Giving Years Shetland and Shetlanders 1939-1945* (Lerwick 1991) p. 316
11. SA4/523/10 October 17 1946
12. Press and broadcast notice Post Office Telecommunications March 21 1975
13. Manson T. M. Y., Council News – No. 16 November 1991 p. 11
14. *The Shetland Times* March 28 1975
15. Historic Scotland Shetland Islands Council Lerwick Burgh Issued 12.08.1996 p. 19
16. Information from Grant Gilfillan, SIC Property and Asset Department
17. Manson Thomas, *Lerwick during the last Half Century* (Lerwick 1923) p. 138
18. Oral information from Thomas Moncrieff
19. *The Shetland News* January 22 1898 *Article Old Lerwick*
20. *The Shetland Times* February 17 1900 p. 4

The Lodberrie
1. Jakobsen Jakob, *The Place-names of Shetland* (London 1936) p. 24
2. Smith Hance D., *Shetland Life and Trade 1550-1914* (Edinburgh 1984) p. 336
3. Irvine James W., *Lerwick the birth and growth of an island town* (Lerwick 1985) p. 53
4. Sandison William, *A Shetland Merchant's Day-Book in 1762* (Lerwick 1934) p. 15
5. Irvine James W., *Lerwick the birth and growth of an island town* (Lerwick 1985) p. 53
6. Manson Thomas, *Lerwick during the last Half Century* (Lerwick 1923) p. 140
7. Discussion with Margaret Stuart Robertson
8. Disposition by Miss Adelaide Beatrice Catherine Hunter in favour of Thomas Moncrieff 1961
9. Disposition by Miss Adelaide Beatrice Catherine Hunter in favour of Thomas Moncrieff 1961
10. Wonders William C., *The Lodberries of Lerwick* Scottish Geographical Magazine vol. III No.2 p. 91 1995
11. *The Shetland Times* Saturday 17 February 1900
12. Manson Thomas, *Lerwick during the last Half Century* (Lerwick 1923) p. 137
13. Oral information from Erik Moncrieff

14. Disposition by Miss Adelaide Beatrice Catherine Hunter in favour of Thomas Moncrieff 1961
15. SA AD22/1011925/26 report concerning the destruction by fire of shop at 22 Commercial Street, occupied by Frederick Irvine, Knowe, Lerwick 30 Nov. 1925; 7 Dec.1925
16. Oral Information from Eunice Paton and Rita Mouat
17. *ibid.*, Peter Smith
18. *ibid.*, Erik Moncrieff

Bain's Court, Raven's Court, Water Lane and Irvinesgord
1. An example of a trance can be seen at the foot of Burns Lane, Commercial Street
2. Tait E. S. Reid, *A Lerwick Miscellany* (Lerwick 1955) p. 4
3. Oral information from Thomas Moncrieff
4. Manson Thomas, *Lerwick during the last Half Century* (Lerwick 1923) p. 137
5. Robertson Margaret Stuart, *Sons and Daughters of Shetland 1800-1900* (Lerwick 1991) p. 10
6. Tait E. S. Reid, *A Lerwick Miscellany* (Lerwick 1955) p. 4
7. *ibid.*
8. The author's recollection
9. *The Shetland News* January 22 1898 *Article Old Lerwick*
10. *The New Shetlander* Yule Number 270 2014
11. SA4/523/1 August 22 1782
12. SA4/523/1 July 3 1829
13. SA4/523/1 September 10 1849
14. Flinn Derek, *Travellers in a bygone Shetland: An Anthology* (Edinburgh 1989) p. 84
15. SA4/523/2 November 14 1866
16. Robertson Margaret Stuart, *Sons and Daughters of Shetland 1800-1900* (Lerwick 1991) p. 89
17. Close personal friend of the author's family

'Stebbagrind's House' or Seafield Court
1. Information from Margaret Stuart Robertson
2. Information from Erling J. F. Clausen 1980
3. Information from Margaret Stuart Robertson
4. SA4/523/1 December 31 1845
5. Information from Erling J. F. Clausen 1980
6. *Mansons' Shetland Almanac 1951* p. XIII
7. Oral information from James Winchester

The Queens Hotel
1. Robertson Margaret Stuart, *Sons and Daughters of Shetland 1800-1900* (Lerwick 1991) p. 72
2. Manson Thomas, *Lerwick during the last Half Century* (Lerwick 1923) pp. 135-136
3. SA SC12/53/7 12 December 1807
4. SA D6/110/3 Memorandum of proposed allotments of the Heritable property of Mr William Hay

5. Nicolson James R., *Hay & Company Merchants in Shetland* (Lerwick 1982) pp. 8-9
6. *ibid.*, p. 13
7. SA4/523/1 July 22 1857
8. Nicolson James R., *Hay & Company Merchants in Shetland* (Lerwick 1982) p. 22
9. SA SC12/53/7 January 23 1836
10. *ibid.*, September 2 1845
11. Manson Thomas, *Lerwick during the last Half Century* (Lerwick 1923) p. 135
12. Robertson Margaret Stuart, *Sons and Daughters of Shetland 1800-1900* (Lerwick 1991) p. 230
13. SA4/523/2 October 8 1866
14. Nicolson James R., *Hay & Company Merchants in Shetland* (Lerwick 1982) p. 115
15. *The Orkney Herald* October 20 1868
16. *Glasgow Herald* June 5 1870
17. SA SC12/6/1871/54 Petition for discharge from sequestration
18. *The Shetland Times* July 8 1872
19. Peace's *Orkney and Shetland, Almanac Advertiser*
20. Nicolson James R., *Lerwick Harbour* (Lerwick 1977) p. 32
21. Robertson Margaret Stuart, *Sons and Daughters of Shetland 1800-1900* (Lerwick 1991) p. 71
22. Irvine James W., *Lerwick the birth and growth of an island town* (Lerwick 1985) p. 197
23. Nicolson James R., *Lerwick Harbour* (Lerwick 1977) p. 187
24. *The Shetland News* December 2 1926
25. *The Shetland Times* June 2 1950
26. SA4/523/10 August 14 1948
27. SA4/523/12 June 19 1956
28. The author's personal experience
29. Personal experience and reminisces of the author
30. Oral information from Olivia Tulloch
31. *The Shetland Times* September 18 1987
32. Oral information from John Tulloch

59 Commercial Street
1. BBCRS 1/9/3 In Aboot da Night with Frank Chadwick 4 December 1985
2. The author's personal memories
3. BBCRS 1/9/3 In Aboot da Night with Frank Chadwick 4 December 1985
4. Discussion with Margaret Stuart Robertson
5. Manson Thomas, *Lerwick during the last Half Century (Lerwick 1923)* p. 8
6. Discussion with Margaret Stuart Robertson
7. SA4/523/1 December 12 1801
8. SA SC12/6/1820/33/1 *Petition for sequestration by William Hay 1820*
9. Flinn Derek, *Travellers in a bygone Shetland: An Anthology* (Edinburgh 1989) p. 83
10. *The Shetland Times* February 20 1892
11. *The Shetland Times* December 17 1898
12. SA Valuation Roll Lerwick 1914-15
13. *Mansons' Shetland Almanac Advertiser 1922* p.xi

14. Manson Thomas, *Lerwick during the last Half Century (Lerwick 1923)* p. 44
15. *Mansons' Shetland Almanac Advertiser 1929* p.xxviii
16. *The Shetland Times* May 9 1952 Advertisement
17. BBCRS 1/9/3 In Aboot da Night with Frank Chadwick 4 December 1985
18. SA Valuation Rolls Lerwick

61-63 Commercial Street
1. Robertson Margaret Stuart, *Sons and Daughters of Shetland 1800-1900* (Lerwick 1991) p. 115
2. *The Shetland Times* March 31 1883 p. 2
3. SA JP33/5/12/16 Plans of premises at 59, 61, & 63 Commercial Street, Lerwick March 20 1906
4. Robertson Margaret Stuart, *Sons and Daughters of Shetland 1800-1900* (Lerwick 1991) pp. 205-206
5. SA Valuation Roll Lerwick 1914-15
6. *ibid.*, 1915-16
7. SA4/523/8 June 3 1928
8. SA4/523/10 December 11 1947
9. SA4/523/11 April 7 1955
10. SA4/523/14 May 8 1968
11. Oral information from Anna Simpson
12. Information courtesy of Charlie Simpson
13. *ibid.*

65 Commercial Street
1. *Mansons' Shetland Almanac Advertiser 1922* p. 214
2. SA4/523/1 Sept. 23 1852
3. SA Census for Lerwick 1851-1881
4. *ibid.*, 1891
5. *The Shetland Times* June 10 1893
6. *The Shetland Times* August 11 1934
7. *The Shetland Times* advertisement June 1 1935
8. SA4/523/13 July 26 1965
9. Oral information from Anna Simpson

Seaview Stores and Seaview House
1. Nicolson James R., *Lerwick Harbour* (Lerwick 1977) p. 29
2. Sandison William, *A Shetland Merchant's Day-Book in 1762* (Lerwick 1934) p. 23
3. Robertson Margaret Stuart, *Sons and Daughters of Shetland 1800-1900* (Lerwick 1991) pp. 132-133
4. Tait E. S. Reid, *A Lerwick Miscellany* (Lerwick 1955) p. 41
5. Shetland Family History Society
6. SASC12/43/3/ p. 15
7. *The Shetland Times* April 12 1884
8. SASC12/43/3/ p. 224
9. SA4/523/4 Disposition by Trustee for behoof of creditors of William James,

lately china merchant and grocer to Daniel Rendall Williamson, merchant
10. *Mansons' Shetland Almanac 1922* p. 19
11. *ibid.*, 1932 p.
12. *Shetland Life* October 1993 pp. 9-10
13. SA Valuation Roll 1964-1965
14. Oral information from Inger Watt
15. SA Valuation Rolls Lerwick 1961-1968
16. Oral information from Anna Simpson

The Old Tolbooth
1. RCAHMS Tolbooths and Town-houses Civic Architecture in Scotland to 1833 (Edinburgh 1996) p. 1
2. Irvine James W., *Lerwick the birth and growth of an island town* (Lerwick 1985) p. 17
3. RCAHMS Tolbooths and Town-houses Civic Architecture in Scotland to 1833 (Edinburgh 1996) p. 134
4. Information from Margaret Stuart Robertson
5. SA Minutes of the Commissioners of Supply Vol. I 1753-1793
6. Sutherland Paul J., *Morton Lodge No. 89, 250 years of a Lerwick Institution 1762-2012* (Lerwick 2012) pp. 18-19
7. RCAHMS Tolbooths and Town-houses Civic Architecture in Scotland to 1833 (Edinburgh 1996) p. 134
8. Sutherland Paul J., *Morton Lodge No. 89, 250 years of a Lerwick Institution 1762-2012* (Lerwick 2012) p. 20
9. SA Minutes of the Commissioners of Supply Vol. I 1753-1793
10. Information from Margaret Stuart Robertson
11. Sutherland Paul J., *Morton Lodge No. 89, 250 years of a Lerwick Institution 1762-2012* (Lerwick 2012) p. 62
12. Crawford James M., *The Parish of Lerwick, 1701-1901* (Lerwick 1901) p. 26
13. RCAHMS Tolbooths and Town-houses Civic Architecture in Scotland to 1833 (Edinburgh 1996) p. 134
14. Graham John J., *A vehement thirst after knowledge* (Lerwick 1998) p. 124
15. RCAHMS Tolbooths and Town-houses Civic Architecture in Scotland to 1833 (Edinburgh 1996) p. 134
16. SA D6/292/4 Lerwick Auld Toon Clock
17. Nelson George, *Reminiscences of the Shetland Fireside* (Sandwick 1977) p. 30
18. Greig P. W., *Annals of a Shetland Parish Delting* (Lerwick 1892) p. 45
19. Shetland Family History Society *Coontin Kin No. 33 Yule 1999* pp. 23-27
20. SA *Second Report of Inspectors of Prisons*. County Gaol Lerwick visited several times between the 17th and 31st of August 1836
21. Smith Brian, *Shetland Folk Book Vol. VIII* (Lerwick 1988) pp. 1-13
22. Sutherland Paul J., *Morton Lodge No. 89, 250 years of a Lerwick Institution 1762-2012* (Lerwick 2012) p. 98
23. Manson Thomas, *Lerwick during the last Half Century (Lerwick 1923)* p. 8
24. "*Da Fishermen's Mission*" *A century of Service in Shetland by the Royal National Mission to Deep Sea Fishermen 1907-2007* (Unst 2007) pp. 9-10
25. Notes from plaque at Toll Clock Shopping Centre

26. SA CO/3/16/1 Minutes of the Civil Defence Committee November 1961-August 1968
27. SA6/493/2/11/3 Plan of Civil Defence Headquarters Lerwick
28. Shetland Islands Council *Official Naming of the Bressay Ferry Leirna* November 14 1992
29. RCAHMS Tolbooths and Town-houses Civic Architecture in Scotland to 1833 (Edinburgh 1996) p. 134
30. The author's personal knowledge
31. *Master Builder The magazine of the Federation of Master Builders* September 2005

Early Schools
1. Graham John J., *A vehement thirst after knowledge* (Lerwick 1998) p. 15
2. *ibid.*, p. 14
3. *ibid.*, p. 123
4. *ibid.*, p. 124
5. *The Shetland Times* July 6 and 13 1907
6. *Centenary of the Anderson Educational Institute History and Personal Reminiscences* (Lerwick 1962) p. 14
7. Spence Catherine *Arthur Anderson His Letters and Literary Remains* (London 1901) pp. 13-17
8. Manson Thomas, *Lerwick during the last Half Century* (Lerwick 1923) p. 224
9. *Excerpts from Minutes of Meetings of Feuars and Heritors of Lerwick* (Lerwick 1909) p. 18
10. Manson Thomas, *Lerwick during the last Half Century* (Lerwick 1923) p. 224
11. *ibid.*, p. 227
12. Leslie John A., *Lerwick Baptist Church, A History* (Brae 1994) pp. 14-15
13. Irvine James W., *Lerwick the birth and growth of an island town* (Lerwick 1985) p. 133
14. *The New Shetlander* No. 114 Yule 1975 p. 11
15. Graham John J., *A vehement thirst after knowledge* (Lerwick 1998) p. 139
16. *Coontin Kin* Shetland Family History Society No. 49 (Lerwick Yule 2003) pp.16-17
17. *The Shetland Times* August 19 1876
18. Taylor Marsali, *Women's Suffrage in Shetland* (Lula, com 2010) p. 70
19. *Centenary of the Anderson Educational Institute History and Personal Reminiscences* (Lerwick 1962) p. 25
20. Irvine James W., *Lerwick the birth and growth of an island town* (Lerwick 1985) p. 186
21. *ibid.*, p. 26
22. *ibid.*, p. 187
23. SA 4/523/7 February 9 1909
24. SA 1/3/8 May 17 1923
25. *Centenary of the Anderson Educational Institute History and Personal Reminiscences* (Lerwick 1962) p. 28-29
26. www.bellsbrae.shetland.sch.uk
27. *Official programme for opening of Extension to Anderson Educational Institute*, May 29 1964
28. www.bellsbrae.shetland.sch.uk ›
29. Irvine James W., *Lerwick the birth and growth of an island town* (Lerwick 1985) pp. 294-295

The 1900 Storm
1. *The Shetland Times* February 17 1900 p. 4
2. *The Shetland News* February 24 1900 p. 4

Da Auld Kirkyard
1. Tait E. S. Reid, *A Lerwick Miscellany* (Lerwick 1955) p. 59
2. The author's personal observation
3. Shetland Family History Society *Monumental Inscriptions Project* (Aberdeen 2003) p. 18
4. Crawford James M., *The Parish of Lerwick, 1701-1901* (Lerwick 1901) p. 68
5. Greig P W., *Annals of a Shetland Parish Delting* (Lerwick 1892) p. 44
6. Crawford James M., *The Parish of Lerwick, 1701-1901* (Lerwick 1901) pp. 15-16
7. Tait E. S. Reid, *A Lerwick Miscellany* (Lerwick 1955) p. 59
8. *The Shetland Times, The Passing of the 'Auld Kirk'* Saturday 25 May; Saturday 1 June and Saturday June 8, 1907
9. Sutherland Paul J., *Morton Lodge No. 89, 250 years of a Lerwick Institution 1762-2012* (Lerwick 2012) pp. 96 & 98
10. Manson Thomas, *Lerwick during the last Half Century (1867-1917)* (Lerwick 1991) pp. 166-168
11. Tait E. S. Reid, *A Lerwick Miscellany* (Lerwick 1955) pp. 58-59
12. *The Shetland Times* Saturday February 4 1893 SA D6/292/6 p. 176
13. Oral information from Queens Lane residents
14. Nicolson James R., *Lerwick Harbour* (Lerwick 1977) p. 163
15. Sutherland Paul J., *Morton Lodge No. 89, 250 years of a Lerwick Institution 1762 -2012* (Lerwick 2012) pp. 190-191
16. *The Shetland Times* Friday May 13 1966 p. 1
17. *The Shetland Times* Friday April 15 1966 p. 6
18. *The Shetland Times* Friday May 13 1966 p1
19. Shetland Family History Society *Monumental Inscriptions Project* (Aberdeen 2003) pp. 18-31
20. Oral information from eyewitnesses, neighbours, men employed in the cemetery, truck drivers and workmen who were involved in clearing the kirkyard
21. Oral information from eyewitness
22. Shetland Family History Society *Monumental Inscriptions 18*, Lerwick (1) (Aberdeen 2001) pp. 33-35

Da Big Kirk
1. Crawford James M., *The Parish of Lerwick, 1701-1901* (Lerwick 1901) pp. 44-46
2. Clausen E. J. F. and Manson Thomas M. Y., *150th Anniversary of Lerwick Parish Church* (Lerwick 1979 p. 3
3. Crawford James M., *The Parish of Lerwick, 1701-1901* (Lerwick 1901) pp. 50-51
4. *ibid.*, p. 53
5. Clausen E. J. F. and Manson Thomas M. Y., *150th Anniversary of Lerwick Parish Church* (Lerwick 1979 p. 4
6. Crawford James M., *The Parish of Lerwick, 1701-1901* (Lerwick 1901) p. 59
7. Clausen E. J. F. and Manson Thomas M. Y., *150th Anniversary of Lerwick Parish Church* (Lerwick 1979) p. 7

8. Crawford James M., *The Parish of Lerwick, 1701-1901* (Lerwick 1901) p. 59
9. Clausen E. J. F. and Manson Thomas M. Y., *150th Anniversary of Lerwick Parish Church* (Lerwick 1979) p. 7
10. Crawford James M., *The Parish of Lerwick, 1701-1901* (Lerwick 1901) p. 61
11. *The Shetland News* June 26 1897
12. Clausen E. J. F. Manson Thomas M. Y., *150th Anniversary of Lerwick Parish Church* (Lerwick 1979) pp. 8-10
13. *ibid.*, p. 19
14. *ibid.*, p. 10
15. *Centenary St Ringan's Church Lerwick Shetland 1886-1986* (Lerwick 1986) p. 6
16. Clausen E. J. F. Manson Thomas M. Y., *150th Anniversary of Lerwick Parish Church* (Lerwick 1979) p. 11
17. *Centenary St Ringan's Church Lerwick Shetland 1886-1986* (Lerwick 1986) pp. 6-8
18. Clausen E. J. F. Manson Thomas M. Y., *150th Anniversary of Lerwick Parish Church* (Lerwick 1979) pp. 19-20
19. *ibid.*, p. 13
20. *Centenary St Ringan's Church Lerwick Shetland 1886-1986* (Lerwick 1986) p. 9
21. *ibid.*, p. 16
22. *St Columba's Church Lerwick, Service of Rededication* Sunday 3rd May 1987
23. *The Shetland Times* August 15 2008
24. *The Shetland Times* December 5 2008
25. *St Columba's Church of Scotland, Lerwick Service of Rededication* Sunday 15th January 2009

St Clement's Church Hall

1. Clausen E. J. F. and Manson Thomas M. Y., *150th Anniversary of Lerwick Parish Church* (Lerwick 1979) p. 8
2. *The Shetland Times* May 20 1911
3. SA D6/292/6/p. 270
4. *The Shetland Times* July 1 1911
5. Clausen E. J. F. and Manson Thomas M. Y., *150th Anniversary of Lerwick Parish Church* (Lerwick 1979) pp. 8-10
6. Irvine James W., *The Giving Years Shetland and Shetlanders 1939-1945* (Lerwick 1991) p. 9
7. County of Zetland Annual Report by Medical Officer of Health Year ending 31 December 1939 p. 11
8. Clausen E. J. F. and Manson Thomas M. Y., *150th Anniversary of Lerwick Parish Church* (Lerwick 1979) pp. 12-13
9. 1st Lerwick Company, The Boy's Brigade, *Golden Jubilee Historical Booklet* (Lerwick 1983) p. 18
10. Islesburgh Management Committee Islesburgh House 1945-1980 (Lerwick 1980) p. 15
11. Islesburgh Exhibition Committee Islesburgh Exhibition 1947-1997 (Lerwick 1997) p. 7
12. Burgess George et al, *The History of Shetland Badminton* (Lerwick 2006) pp. 5-6
13. Up-Helly-Aa Programmes 1968 and 1989

14. Historic Scotland Shetland Islands Council Lerwick Burgh Issued 12.08.1996 p. 159
15. *The Shetland Times* October 21 2014
16. *The Shetland News* January 7 2016

The Church of Scotland Canteen
1. Nicolson James R., *Lerwick Harbour* (Lerwick 1977) p. 129
2. Nicolson James R., *Shetland And Oil* (London 1975) p. 38
3. SA D50/15/3 Memo about Dispatch Rider Letter Service which highlights camps
4. Nicolson James R., *Lerwick Harbour* (Lerwick 1977) p. 129
5. Irvine James W, *Lerwick the birth and growth of an island town* (Lerwick 1985) Illustration 63
6. SA CH2/1071/110 p. 286
7. *West Word the community paper for Mallaig, Morar, Arisaig, Lochailort, Glenfinnan, Glenuig, Knoygart and the Small Isles*, October 2003
8. SA CO5/2/38 ZCC Library Sub-Committee
9. *The Shetland Times* June 29 1966
10. Clausen E. J. F. and Manson Thomas M. Y., *150th Anniversary of Lerwick Parish Church* (Lerwick 1979) p. 15

Early Lerwick Inns and Hotels
1. Information from Margaret Stuart Robertson
2. SA SC12/6/1820/33/1
3. Flinn Derek, *Travellers in a bygone Shetland: An Anthology* (Edinburgh 1989) p. 83
4. Robertson Margaret Stuart, *Sons and Daughters of Shetland 1800-1900* (Lerwick 1991) p. 180
5. Flinn Derek, *Travellers in a bygone Shetland: An Anthology* (Edinburgh 1989) p. 91
6. *The Shetland Times* February 20 1892
7. Reid John T., *Art Rambles in Shetland* (Edinburgh 1869) p. 3
8. Manson Thomas, *Lerwick during the last Half Century (1867-1917)* (Lerwick 1991) p. 9
9. *The Shetland Times* December 24 1987
10. *John o' Groat Journal* June 8 1871
11. Manson Thomas, *Lerwick during the last Half Century (1867-1917)* (Lerwick 1991) p. 10
12. Ployen Christian, *Reminiscences of a voyage to Shetland, Orkney & Scotland* (Lerwick 1896) p. 9
13. *ibid.*, p.14
14. *The Shetland Times* January 4 1890
15. SA CO/6/20 Poorhouse and County Homes records 1884-1962
16. Flinn Derek, *Travellers in a Bygone Shetland An Anthology* (Edinburgh 1989) p. 231
17. Robertson Margaret Stuart, *Sons and Daughters of Shetland 1800-1900* (Lerwick 1991) p. 116
18. Census 1871
19. *The Shetland Times* October 19 1871
20. *The Orkney and Shetland Directory Advertiser* p. 153
21. *Peace's Orkney and Shetland Almanac Advertiser*

22. *The Orkney and Shetland Directory advertiser*
23. *Peace's Orkney and Shetland Almanac Advertiser*
24. Manson Thomas, *Lerwick during the last Half Century* (Lerwick 1923) p. 62
25. SA JP33/5/12/3 Plan of Royal Bar
26. *The Shetland Times* October 11 1930
27. *The Shetland Times* May 31 1890

Smugglers' Tunnels, or Cellars?
1. Irvine Fred, *Shetland's Believe it or Not* (Lerwick 1952) No. 1
2. Irvine Fred, *Pictures from Shetland's Past* (Lerwick 1955)
3. SA CE85 *Letter Books Collector to Board no. 12*, 24 March 1798
4. Oral information Betty Simpson
5. Manson Thomas, *Lerwick during the last Half Century (Lerwick 1923)* p. 139
6. Oral information from Maurice Manson
7. Oral information from Mary Williamson
8. Personal experience of the author
9. Correspondence with Ian Jamieson
10. Oral information from Ian Barrie
11. Irvine Fred, *Shetland's Believe it or Not* (Lerwick 1952) No. 30
12. Personal experience of the author
13. Information from Margaret Stuart Robertson
14. Robertson Margaret Stuart, *Sons and Daughters of Shetland 1800-1900* (Lerwick 1991) p. 165
15. Information from Margaret Stuart Robertson
16. Irvine Fred, *Shetland's Believe it or Not* (Lerwick 1952) No. 17
17. Oral information from Andrew Williamson
18. Oral information from Thomas Moncrieff
19. Oral information from Noelle Gordon
20. Personal experience of the author
21. Oral information from Bruce Scott
22. Manson Thomas, *Lerwick during the last Half Century (Lerwick 1923)* p. 135
23. Robertson Margaret Stuart, *Sons and Daughters of Shetland 1800-1900* (Lerwick 1991) p. 136
24. Oral information from Erling J. F. Clausen
25. *The Shetland Times* February 21 1952 p. 4
26. Discussion with Joe Gray
27. Irvine Fred, *Shetland's Believe it or Not* (Lerwick 1952) No. 44
28. Oral Information from Thomas Moncrieff
29. *The Shetland News* December 15 1932 p. 4
30. Robertson Margaret Stuart, *Sons and Daughters of Shetland 1800-1900* (Lerwick 1991) p. 191
31. Smith Hance D., *Shetland Life and Trade 1550-1914* (Edinburgh 1984) p. 100
32. *The Shetland News* October 8 1904 p. 4
33. Oral Information from John Evans
34. Tait E. S. Reid, *A Lerwick Miscellany* (Lerwick 1955) p. 12
35. Oral Information from Jim Henry

36. Sandison William, *A Shetland Merchant's Day-Book in 1762* (Lerwick 1934) p. 71
37. *The Shetland News* June 30 1932 p. 4
38. *The Shetland Times* February 11 1955 p. 4
39. Oral Information from Clive Henderson
40. Irvine Fred, *Shetland's Believe it or Not* (Lerwick 1952) No. 51
41. Manson Thomas, *Lerwick during the last Half Century (Lerwick 1923)* p. 69
42. Personal knowledge of author
43. Personal knowledge of author

INDEX

Page numbers in *italics* refer to captions.

Aberdeen, William xv
Adamson, William 108
Aitken, John M. 25, 26, 29, 63–4, 114, 122
Albert Café/Hall 6, 9–10, *10*, 124
Albert Court 124
Albert Hotel 9, 124
Alexandra Wharf 34
Alfonso, King of Spain 40
Allan, Lessel 79
Anderson, Arthur *36*, 37–40, 100
Anderson, Mrs C. 91
Anderson Educational Institute/High School *15*, 23–4, *23*, 25, 26, *38*, 39, 100, 102, 103, 104
Anderson, Elizabeth 26
Anderson Homes *15*, 39, *39*, 56
Anderson, Joan 90
Anderson, L. & M. 73
Anderson, Mark 86
Anderson, Robert 62, 90
Anderson, Thomas 42, 62
Anderson, Tom 57
Anglo-Scottish herring station 57
Angus, Gilbert 132
Angus, Leslie *21*
Angus, P. L. *130*
Angus's Closs *131*, 132
Ann Scollay's Closs 51
Annsbrae House 29
Arcus, Barbara 42
Arthur, Laurence and Stanley 47
Ashley, John 33
Auld Kirk xvi, 11, 45, 48, 94, 96, 100, 108, 113
Auld Kirkyard 71, 107–12, *107*, *110*, *111*, *112*

Bain, Gilbert 70, *70*
Bain, James *5*, 69, 70
Bain's Beach xv, 66, 69, *74*, *75*, 76
Bain's Court xvi, *64*, 69–72, *69*
Baird, Rev. George W. 120
Bannatyne, John 62

Baptist manse 53, 100, 101
Barclay, Rev. Thomas 114
Barrie, George *63*
Bayne, Rev. and Mrs. Alexander A. 46, 47
Bellevue Camp 24
Bell's Brae school 103, 104
Betjeman, Sir John 29, 80
Bewick, James 123
Binns, W. D. C. 137
Blance, Mary 49
Böd of Gremista *36*, 100
Bolt, Mrs Grace 57
Bolt, Jane 15, *15*
Bolt, Thomas 39, 57, 93
Bouwmeister, Mrs 123
Brand, Rev. John 11
Bressay Sound/Lerwick Harbour 1, 2, 4, *4*, *5*, *6*, 39, *40*, 57, 115
Brevik House 122
Brock, Barbara 13
Broun, J. C. C. 62
Brown, James 42
Brown, John 53, 57
Brown, John Arcus 42
Brown, Margaret Gillie 42
Brown, William 82, *82*
Brown's Buildings and Brown's Road 53
Bruce Hostel 24, 25–6, *25*
Bruce, John, of Sumburgh 16, 18, 94
Bruce, Robert H. 18, 24, 25, 26
Bruce, T. L. 117
Bullet Loan *see* Knab Road
Burgess, Jim 92
Burgess Street *141*
Burns Lane xvi, 13, 135
Byrne, John 9, 124
Byrne's Temperance Hotel 124, *124*

Cadell, Kirstie 95
Calderhead's Brae 102
Calderhead's School 101, *101*, 102–3
Cameron, Margaret Anne 31
Cameron, Mary Margaret 29–30
Cameron, Major Thomas Mouat 29
Campbell, Rev. A. J. 6, 117
Campbell, Alex. 137
Campbell, Dorothea Primrose 71

Campbell, Eliza Matilda 71
Chadwick, Lillian and Frank 81, 83, 138
Chalmers, Margaret 53
Chalmers, Mr and Mrs William 16, 53
Chapel House/Rechabite Hall 102, 116
Charlotte House 53
Charlotte Place 53
    Harry's Department Store 53, 133, 138
    Save the Children shop 124, 138
Charlotte Street 137
Charlotte Street Mission Hall/Havly 34, 35–6, *35*
Cheyne, Sir W. Watson 34
Christie, Helen *56*
Christine Mary, Sister 31
Chromate Lane 105, 128, 138
Church of Jesus Christ of Latter-day Saints *101*, 102, 103
Church Lane 12, 87, 88, 95, 108, 109, *109*, 113, 122
Church Road 87, 113
    car park 107, 111, *112*
    demolitions for 15, 86, 88, 90, 92, *92*, 106, *109*, 135
    underground passage *129*, 130
    see also Auld Kirkyard
Church of Scotland Canteen 119–20, *119*
Circus Camp 119, *119*
Clairmont Place 53, *99*, 100, 101, 137
Clark, J. R. S. 28
Clark, James 95
Clickimin 104, 106, 118
Clifford, Alice Geraldine 62
Clumlie 57, 114, *114*
Coastguard Houses 15, *18*, 19, *19*, 20
Cockstool/Cockstool Rock 89, 90
Coffee House 5–6, 9–10, 124
Commercial Bank 130–1, *130*
Commercial Hotel 124
Commercial Street
    2-8 (Copland's House) *46*, 51, *51*, *54*, 65, *126*
    7 xvi, *46*, *47*
    9 (Old Manse) xvi, 45–9, *45*, *46*, *47*, *49*, *54*, 67, 105, 121
    10 (Torrie's House) xvi, 16, 42, 45, *46*, 51, *52*, 53, *54*, 65, 89
    11 *46*, *54*
    12 *51*, *127*
    15 51, 52, *52*, 53, *54*, 83
    14 (MacBeath's House/Sea Door) *127*
    17 (Da Roost Hoose) 51, *51*, 52, *52*, 53, *54*, *127*
    36 (Seaview Stores) 86, 88, 89–92, *89*, *90*, *91*, *92*, *96*, 130, 135

Commercial Street Cont.
   36a 86, 91
   42-44 (Solotti's/Faerdie-Maet) 96, 120, 134, 135, 138
   49 (Seafield Court) 73–4, *74*, 122, 128, *128*
   51 (Willie Plenty's/Spider's Web) 82, *82*
   59 (Sinclair's Tavern/Hairy Ned's/Hygienic/From Shetland With Love) 52, 78, 81–4, *83*, 85, *86*, 98, 121, 138
   60-62 (Anderson & Co) 62
   61 (Smith & Co/Vaila Fine Art) 85, 86, *86*, *87*, *89*, 138
   61-63 83, 85–6, *85*, *86*, 87, 90, 92
   65 (Economy Corner) 15, *86*, 87–8, *87*, 90, *92*
   67 (Shetland Antiques) 122
   74-78 (Herd's/Conochie's/the Roost) 5, 131, 137–8, *138*
   77 (Shetland Times Bookshop) 94, 122
   80-82 (Reid Tait's/Co-op/Ninian & Aurora) 5, 131–2, 142, *142*
   84 (Angus's/Georgeson's/Fat Little Pony) 132, 137, *138*
   86 (W. A. Robertson/Da Noost) 132, 133, 135
   92 (Gift Shop/Rae's) 123, 133, 137
   96 (Inkster's/Medical Hall/Loose Ends) 4, 137
   97 (Lerwick Hotel/Smith's of Lerwick) xvi, 108, 122
   98 (Stove & Smith/Scottish Hydro-Electric) 133, 136
   125-127 (Lerwick Meat Co/Red Cross) 97, 138
   133 (Leys) 141, *142*
   143 (Bayes) 122, 132
   155 (old Quendale House/Ollason's/Stage Door) 62, 133, 137
   169-171 (Sinclair's/N-graved & Parliamentary Office) 137
   173 (hotel/Royal Bar/supermarkets/Boots) *123*, 124, 135, 141, *142*
   after 1900 gale 64, 66, 105, 106
   Anderson, T. J./Tourist Office 135
   cart access 53
   Miss Chalmers Stairs 53
   Citizens Advice Bureau (CAB) *74*
   Co-op
       80-82 (now Ninian & Aurora) 5, 131–2, 142, *142*
       M&Co 40, *132*, 133, *134*, 135, 137
   Dutch in 2, 4, *5*, 7, 11, *96*
   Flower Shop 135
   R. Goudie & Son/The Wine Shop xvi, 136, *136*
   Grand Hotel 18, 52, 59, 80, 122–3, *123*, 124, 132
   Greenwald's/Klaize 133, 137, *137*
   Halcrows Restaurant 138
   Hayfield Court xvi, 45, 51, *51*, *54*, *55*, 56, *126*, *127*
   inns and hotels 121–4
   W. R. Jamieson's/Laing's 137, 138
   Cecilia Johnson's cottage *52*
   Kay's/Begg Shoes and Bags 123, 135

  'Keetie Bruce's'/Da Fish Bowl 135, *135*, 136–7, *136*
  Kelday's Court 122, 132–3
  Knowe xv, *15*, 41–4, *41*, *54*, 67, 125
  Peter Leisk's/High Level Music Centre 135, 138, *138*
  Lodberrie 43, 46, *61*, *64*, 65–8, *65*, *66*, *67*, 69, 105, 128
  Malcolmson & Co/Aa Fired Up 137
  Alex. Manson/Mirrie Dancers Chocolatier xvi, 135, *137*
  Jas. Manson 135
  Miller Opticians 85
  Old Rock Cafe 138
  Peterson & Co 138
  Porteous/Bank of Scotland 137
  R. & C.'s/Camera Shop xvi, 11, 135
  Royal Bank of Scotland 130–1, *130*
  Scottshall Court 42, *74*, 75
  Seawinds *74*
  Shetland Bookshop *130*
  'the Shore' xv
  James S. Smith/Continental Tastes 137, *137*
  smugglers' facilities 65, 75, 125–34
  Stout's Court 42, 51–4, *54*, *60*, 83, 114, 121, 126, 127
  Thomas Stout's house 52, 122
  Tatties & Point 138
  Universal Stores 135–6
  see also Charlotte Place; Queens Hotel
Comper, Sir Ninian 29, 30, 31, 32
Congregational Church 99
Connon, James 77
Conroy, Bob *58*
Copland, James 65
Copland's House *46*, 51, *51*, *54*, 65, *126*
Cork and Orrery, Earl of 24, 26
County Buildings 63, 96, 110
County Library 120, *120*
  see also Shetland Library
Courtney, Janet 27, 28
Coutts, Alexander 122
Coutts, Beth, Celie, and Ewen *21*
Coutts, Dennis 41–2, 43, *43*, 58, 133
Coutts, Ian 41
Coutts, Muriel 43, *43*
Cowie, Dr John 13
Cowie, William 124
Cowie's Hotel 124
Craigie, Catherine 61–2
Craigie, Elizabeth 46, 62

Craigie, Mrs Elizabeth 61
Craigie, James 46, 61, 62, 73
Craigie, Capt. John 46, 61, 62
Craigie, Margaret 46
Craigie, Robert 73
Craigie Stane xv, 46, *61*, 64, *64*, *65*, 66, 67, 105
Craigie, William *47*
Craigie's Court xvi, 61–4
Craigie's Well 42
Crutwell, Mrs Lilias Greig 122
Curle, A. O. 40
Customs House 69, 94
Cuthbert, James and Dorothy 49

Datema, Dom S. 6, 117–18
Davidson, Alexander and John 71
Davies, E. Salter 27, 28
Deans, Admiral 2
Dick family, Fracafield 70
Dick, William 45
Djunkowsky, Dr Stephan de 122
Draw-well Closs 70
Drill Hall 140, *141*
Duke's Neb *41*, 43
Dulk, J. den *8*
Duncan, Andrew 99
Duncan, Mrs Violet 84
Duncan, Walter, snr 41
Dundas, Sir Laurence 16
Dutchman's Leap 3, *3*
Duthie family, Kveldsro House 57

Edinburgh, Margaret 61
Ellesmere House *105*
Ellesmere Stores 135
Esplanade *9*, 40, 65, 66, 89, 92, *92*, 105–6, *105*, 109, 133
    see also Tolbooth
Ethel, Sister 31
Eunson, Mrs Christina 91
Eunson, William 141–2
Evans, Thomas 76–7

Farmer, Gordon, Patricia and Peter *21*
Farquhar, William 94
Fea, Magnus 93
Fever/Smallpox Hospital 11–14, *11*, *14*

Fleurti, Margaret 46–7
Flying Angel, The 33–6, *33*
Forbes, Colin 49
Forbes, Robert and James 93
Fordyce, Charlie 123
Fordyce, Samuel 16
Fort Charlotte xvi, 2, 5, 21, 31, 53, 90, 94, 95, 96
Foulis, J. W. 86
Fox, HMS 21, 24, *54*, 62
Franklin, Sir John and Lady 123
Fraser, John 18

Gallie, Bobbie *21*
Galloway, James K. 16
Ganson, E. Hilda 116
Ganson, Jim 133, *134*
Garriock, A. J. 96
Garrison Theatre 140, *141*
Garthspool/Garthspool Place 9
Garthspool Reading Room 9
Garthspool Road 5–6, 9–10, 124
Gibson, Richard and Victoria 45
Gifford, John 107
Gifford, Thomas, of Busta 99
Gilbert Bain Hospital 14, 24, 26, 31, 36, 70
Gilbertson family, 12 St Magnus Street 72
Gilbertson Park 5, 115, 119
Gilbertson Road 70
Gilbertson, Robert P. 115
Gillie, George 42
Gillie's Pier *46*, 65, 105
Glass, John G. 100
Glen Orchy House 29, *29*, 32
Glenlea, Ronald Street 87
Gordon, Miss (teacher) 100
Gordon, Alexander 124
Grahame, Mary 33, 34
Grand Hotel 18, 52, 59, 80, 122–3, *123*, 124, 132
Grantfield 34, *34*, 63
Gray, Joe *129*, 130
Gray, Laurence 41
Gray, Magnus 71
Green, Margaret 61
Greenfield *see* Clumlie; St Magnus Church; Walker's School
Greenrig House 48, *114*, 126–7
Greig, Mr 124

Greig's Closs 133
Gressy Loan 15, *17*, 19–22, *19*
Grieg's Lodberry 66
Grierson, Sir Herbert J. C. 62
Grierson, James and Andrew John 62
Grierson, James C. 16
Grierson's Closs/Quendale Lane 62, 131
Grootje's Poortje (Grandmother's Gate) 7, *8*
Grootveld, Henk 8
Gulland, Janet 102
Gutteres, Miss 31

Half Nyepkin xvi, 81, *81*, 82, *83*, *85*
Hangcliff Lane 100, 122, 137
Harbour Street 40, 141
Harris, Albert 78, 83
Harrison, John 67
Harrison Square *131*, 132
Harry's Department Store 53, 65, 133, 138
Havly 35, *35*, 36, *36*
Hay & Company 24, 55, 56, 57, 62, 76, 78
    grocer shop *81*, 82–3, *82*, *83*, 85, *85*, *86*, 121
Hay & Ogilvy 55, 73, 75–6
Hay, Arthur James 55, *55*, 56, 57, 76, 77–8, 82
Hay, Charles 55, 76
Hay, Mrs Charlotte 56
Hay, Elsie B. 28
Hay, George H. B. 55, 56, 76, *76*, 77, 121
Hay, James 75, 82
Hay, John (Jock) Westwood 57
Hay, Margaret Elizabeth 56–7, *57*, 78, 86
Hay, Col. Westwood Norman 57, 78
Hay, William 53, 55, 75–6, 87
Hayfield Court xvi, 45, 51, *51*, *54*, *55*, 56, *126*, *127*
Hayfield Estate 55, 56, 57, 78, 86
Hayfield Hotel 83
Hayfield House 55, 56, 57, 62, 76
Hay's Corner 82
Hay's Lodberry 75, *76*, 98, 129
Hay's Steps *76*
Henderson, Alexander 77
Henderson, Bertha, Grace, and Marlene *21*
Henderson, Christina 42
Henderson, Elizabeth 61
Henderson, John 95
Henderson, Tom 48–9

Henry family
    Twageos House 18
    Yates's Lodberry 76, 78, *78*
Henry, Irene 123
Henry, Mrs Jemima 123
Henry, Jim 8
Henry, John and Robert 76
Herning, Derick 8
Hibbert, Samuel 121
Hill Lane xvi, 13, 131
Hill, Mary Ann 39
Hillhead 48, 102, 118, 120, 131
Hodge, Chris 118
Holland, Charlie *58*
Horse's Head 21
House of Charity 29–32, *29*
Hoversta Dairy 97
Hunter, Beatrice 67, *71*, 72
Hunter, James 100, 101
Hunter, Mrs James 101
Hunter, William Irvine 67
Hyslop, Mr 15
Hyslop's Cottage 15, 87

Infant School Brae 102
Infant Schools *101*, 102, 103
Ingram, Mrs 9
Inkster & Jamieson (Hairy Neds) 52, 83
Inkster, Edward 52, 83
Inkster, George 4
Inkster, Jim 83, *127*
Innes, Peter 82
Innes, Walter 99
Irvine, Andrew 42
Irvine, Fred 42–3, *42*, *54*, 67, 69, 125, 130
    work *44*, *125*, *130*, *132*, 133
Irvine, George *21*, *22*, 73
Irvine, Hilda 73
Irvine, Joe 73
Irvine, John 67, 72
Irvine, Mrs Margaret *22*
Irvine, William 67, 71
Irvinesgord 66, 67, 69–72, *70*, 128
Irving, Leslie and Marcia 49
Isaacson, James 16
Isbister, Tommy 41–2

Islesburgh Community Centre 102
Islesburgh House 118
Isolation Hospital 14

Jakobsen, Jakob 4
James, Capt. William 90
Jamieson, Andrew and Bertie 47
Jamieson, Christina 16–17, *17*
Jamieson, Joan 138
Jamieson, Margaret 52, *52*
Jamieson, Robert 47
Jamieson, W. R. 138
Jamieson's Knitwear *91*, 92
Janet Courtney Hostel *16*, 24, 27–8, *27*
Jeannie Bult's house 15, *15*
John Brown's Station 57
Johnson, Mrs Cecilia *52*
Johnson, Mrs Christina 84
Johnson Cottage *101*
Johnson, Dolly 79
Johnson family, The Lodberrie 67
Johnson, Marjory 79
Johnston, Elizabeth *74*
Johnston, Jesma, John, and Margaret 21

Kay, Theodore 123
Kelday, Mr and Mrs James 132–3
Kelday, John 132
Kelday's Court 122, 132–3
Kerr, Jim 79
King Erik House 120
King George V Playing Fields 119, *119*
King Harald Street 70, 101, 102
Klondyke Cottages *10*
Knab Camp 21, 24, 119
Knab Road 19, 21
    Glen Orchy House 29, *29*, 32
    House of Charity 29–32, *29*
    Old Cemetery 2, 13, 57, 108, 110, 111, *111*
Knab, the 2, *19*, 20, 21, 40
    cemetery 4, 8, *8*, 13, *19*, 21, 110
    Dutchman's Leap 3, *3*
    Smallpox/Fever Hospital 11–14, *11*, *14*
    WWII army camp 21, 24, 119
Knowe, The xv, *15*, 41–4, *41*, *54*, 67, 125
Krinigill 107, *111*, 122

Kveldsro *54*, 55–60, *55*, *56*, *57*, *58*, *60*, 80, *114*

Lamont, Daniel 26
Laurenson, Arthur 63
Laurenson, John William 24
Laurie, John (Jock) 84
Law Lane xvi, 62, 124
Lawrence, Beryl and Rosie *21*
Leask, Charles and Thomas 122
Leask, John Bruce 9
Leask, Joseph 9, 73, 122
Leask's Lodberry 66, *105*
Lendrum, Harriette 31
Leog xvi, *15*, 41, *47*, 48, 53, *54*, 65, 91, 105, *114*
Leog House *54*
Lerwick Central Public School 23, 26, 102, *102*, 103, *103*, 122
Lerwick Combination Hospital 14
Lerwick Harbour/Bressay Sound 1, 2, 4, *4*, *5*, *6*, 39, *40*, 57, 115
Lerwick Hotel 59, 122
Lerwick Parish Church 5–6, 10, 47, 107, 117–18
    see also Auld Kirk; St Clement's Hall; St Columba's Church; St Olaf's Church/Hall
Lerwick Public School *see* Calderhead's School
Levack, Mr *77*, 85, *85*
Leys, Alexander A. 141, *142*
Lie, Inger 90
Lillie, John S. 141
Linklater, George 66
Linklater, James 66, 71
Linklater, Robert 124
Lochend House/Spider's Web xvi, 69, *69*, 70, *74*, 128, 129
Lodberrie 43, 46, *61*, *64*, 65–8, *65*, *66*, *67*, 69, 105, 128
Longmuir, George 120
Lounge Bar 9, 43, 124
Lovers Loan 24, 39, *54*, *114*
Low, Rev. George 2
Lyall, John B. 100

McAlpine, Ian *21*
McCartney, Paul and Linda 80
McDonald, Alistair and Laurna 48
MacDonald, Dr 26
MacDougall, W. L. 25
MacFarlane, Andrew 100
McHattie, Alison *58*
McKay, John 83, 85

McKay, Robert 91
McKinven, Rev. John 16
Macleod, Rev. John 16
McMillan, James 86
McMorine, John 94–5, 99, 100
McNab, Charles 99
McPherson, Mrs Jean *74*
McShane, Felix 90
McWhirter, Mrs Queenie 137
Mair, Joe 57
Malcolmson, Laurence 86
Mansefield 57
Manson, Magnus 41
Manson, Dr T. Mortimer Y. 122
Manson, Thomas 122
Mareel 57
Market Cross xvi, 9, 137, 138
Market House/Market Street 40, 142
Masonic Hall 107, 108, 109, 111, *111*, 113
Mattinson, Mrs Sarah 124
Meeting House 10, *127*, 128
Menzies, Rev. John 99–100
Merrylees, William 13, 122
Methodist Church 57, *101*, 102, 114
Middlebie Hill 119
Midgarth *see Fox*, HMS
Midgarth House 24, *56*
Midgarth Maternity Annexe 24, *24*
Miller, W. 32
Milne, Rev. James 45
Missions to Seamen Institute 33–6, *33*
Mitchell, Alexander 15, 20
Moar, Charlie 141
Moira, Richard 55
Moncrieff family, The Lodberrie 67–8, *68*
Monk, Admiral 2
Morgan, Rev. John 114
Morton, Earl of 15–16, 53, 93
Morton Lodge 16, 94, 96, 99, 108, 109
Mouat, James and Peter 89
Mouat, Robert 16
Mouat, William 94
Mouat's Lodberry 90
Mounthooly Street 35, *36*, 53, 85, *99*, 100, 102, 116
    Lounge Bar 9, 43, 124
Mowat, John 94

Mullay, John 46, 121
Murray, John 75, 129
Murray, Mrs Ruby *56*
Murray's Hol 75, 129, *129*
Murray's Lodberry 126

Navy Lane 61
Neven-Spence, Sir Basil 27
Nice Court *see* Hayfield Court
Nice, Thomas 45
Nicol, Sergeant 95
Nicol, Barbara 52
Nicol's Hotel 95
Nicolson, Arthur 42, 55, 69, 70, 93
Nicolson's Closs 133
Norna's Court xvi
Nort Kirk Closs *see* Queens Lane
North Lodberry 65
North Road 6, 34, 133, 140, *141*, 142
Norwegian Welfare Centre 35–6, *35*

O'Brien, John and Margaret 122
O'Connor, Carol and Patrick 49
Ogilvy, Charles 51, 52, 73, 75
Old Cemetery, Knab Road 2, 13, 57, 108, 110, 111, *111*
Old Manse xvi, 45–9, *45*, *46*, *47*, *49*, *54*, 67, 105, 121
Old Rock Cafe 138
Ollason, Robert 133, 137
Ovington, Mr & Mrs 62

Papa Stour Sword Dancers *17*
Parochial School *99*, 100
Paterson, RSM 120
Paton, Eunice *21*
Paton family, The Lodberrie 67
Paton, Robert 97
Pearson, James 10
Pearson, Morris and Nancy *21*
Peterson, Beth *63*
Peterson, Mimie, Jack, and Bobby *74*
Petrie, P. E. 124
Pig Street *141*
Pirate Lane 9, 124
Pitcairn, Barbara 107–8
Pitt Lane xvi, 122, 131
Ployen, Christian 122

Pochin, Lt. James W. 31, *31*, *32*
Post Office xv, 53, 62, 66, 96, *97*, *106*
Prince Alfred Street 102, 103
Prospect House 62

Queens Hotel 59, *74*, 75–80, *75*, *77*, *78*, *79*, *80*, *81*, *82*, *83*, *91*, 94, 105, 121, *121*, 124
    Bar 79, 83, 85
    café 84
    lodberries and 62, 73, 75, 76, 78, *78*, 126
    passage under 129, 130
Queens Lane 53, 107, *107*, 108, *109*, 110, *111*, *112*, 113, 122
Quendale House 46, 61–4, *61*, 62, *63*, 71, 105
Quendale Lane/Grierson's Closs 62, 131

Ramsay, Robert 99, 108
Raven's Court xvi, 69–72, *69*, *70*, 128, *128*
Reade, Lieut. John and Mrs Joan 22
Reade, Pat *21*
Rechabite Hall/Chapel House 102, 116
Rectory, the *114*
Reform Lane 138, 141
Reid, John T. 122
Rhind, Bill 20
Richan, William 45
RNLI 84, *84*, 97, 98, *98*, 99
RNMDSF 33, *91*, 96
Robertson, Ann 89
Robertson family, Kveldsro Cottage 56, *56*
Robertson, Gideon T. B. 47
Robertson, Gilbert 56, *57*
Robertson, Mrs Jean 89
Robertson, Jenny, Mary, and Zegena *21*
Robertson, Bailie John 66, 67
Robertson, Mary *21*, 91
Robertson, William 89
Robertson's Lodberrie 67
Roost, the 5, 131
Roost Hoose, Da 51, 52, 53, 54, 127
Ross Court xvi, 127, *127*
Ross, James and Irene 49
Ross, Margaret 46
Ross, William and John 127
Rowland, Richard 86
Royal Buildings 124
Royal Hairdressing Saloons *84*
Royal Hotel/Royal Bar *123*, 124, 141

Russell, Thomas 141
Rychlik, Dorota 86

St Clement's Hall 6, 10, 115, 117–18, *117*, 119, *119*
St Columba's Church 51, 108, 113–16, *113*, *115*, 117–18
St Magnus Church 29, *30*, 31, 32, *32*, 34, *34*, 35, 101–2, *101*, 108, *114*, 126
St Magnus Home *see* House of Charity
St Michael's Mission Hall 34, *34*
St Olaf's Church/Hall *110*, 114, 115, 116
St Ringan's Church 115, 116
Sandison, David Hunter 139
Sandison, F. J. 140, *141*
Sandison, George *58*
Sandison, Mary 108
Sands, Barbara 71
Sands' Court 70
   see also Bain's Court
Sands, Rev. James 16, 70
Sands, Jane 66, 71
Sands, Wilhelmina 46
Scalloway Road 70, 101, *101*
Scollay, Ann 51
Scollay, Patrick 45, 65
Scott, Mrs Bella 73
Scott, Elizabeth 129
Scott, Sir Walter 71, 82, 94, 121
Scottshall Court 42, *74*, 75, 129
Sea Road 11, *106*
Seafield Court 73–4, *74*, 122, 128, *128*
Seamen's Church of St Peter 34, *35*, 36
Seamen's Home *91*, *92*, *105*, 106, *106*
Seaview House 90–2, *90*, *91*, *92*, *101*, *106*
Seaview Stores 86, 88, 89–92, *89*, *90*, *91*, *92*, *96*, 130, 135
Setrice, Leslie *58*
Shaw, Rosemary *58*
Shearer, Lt Col Magnus 28
Sherman, George 79
Shetland Hotel 59
Shetland Library 116, 118, 120
Shetland Textile Museum *37*
Simpson, Rita *58*
Sinclair, Arthur, Ian, and Isobel *21*
Sinclair, Bruce 73
Sinclair, Dorothy *90*
Sinclair, Douglas *21*, 41
Sinclair, Douglas M. 8, *90*

Sinclair, Eddie 137
Sinclair, George 77
Sinclair and Hardie 83, 114, 126
Sinclair, Henry 83
Sinclair, James 52, 53
Sinclair, Margaret 8
Sinclair, Nicol 75
Sinclair, Walter 82, 121
Sinclair, Capt. William and Mrs Marion *47*
Sinclair, Col. William, of Ustaness 2
Sinclair, William N. 47, 48
Sinclair's Beach *97, 106*
Sinclair's Pier and Lodberry *105*
Sinclair's Tavern 82, 121
Skene, Danus 49
Skippadock/Skibbadock 4
Slater, Mrs 122
Sletts *101*, 106
Smallpox/Fever Hospital 11–14, *11, 14*
Smith, Very Rev. Dr 115
Smith, Andrew 10, 122
Smith, Anna *58*
Smith, Bill *87, 90*
Smith, Hendry 108
Smith, James J. 90
Smith, Laurence 86, 87, 90, 136
Smith, Mrs Mary 84, 86
Smith, William C. 86, 90
Smythe, John 121
Sound school 104
South Kirk Closs *see* Church Lane
South Ness House 15, *19*, 20, *20, 21*
South Ness Park 13
Spence, Balfour and James R. 131
Spence, Elizabeth 115
Spence, Gilbert W. 12–13
Stane Hoose, Da 9
Steamers' Store Lodberry 66, *66*
Stebbagrind's House *see* Seafield Court
Stephen, Major A. 40
Sterling, Sir Jeffrey *37*
Stevenson, Albert 138
Stevenson, Annie 31
Stewart, Nancy and Mrs Margaret 122
Stout, Barbara 52
Stout, Charles B. 137

Stout, Grizel 53
Stout, John 73
Stout, Robert 51, 53, *54*, 113, 114
Stout, Sir Robert 51, 53, 94, 114
Stout, Thomas 51–2, 53, 83, 94, 114, 122
Stout, William 51, 52, 53, *54*, 113
Stout's Court 42, 51–4, *54*, *60*, 83, 114, 121, 126, 127
Stout's House 126, *126*
    Commercial Street 52, 122
Stout's Pier 51, 65, 105
Strong, John 87
Strong, Thomas 15, 87, 88, 97
Strong's Court 87
Strong's House 15, *15*, 87
Subscription School 99–100
Sutherland, Algar 96
Sutherland, Alice *21*
Sutherland, Laurence 108
Swanson, Donald and Stanley 78–9

Taing House *106*
Tait, Mrs Ann 124
Tait, E. S. Reid *5*, 43, 120, 131–2, 142, *142*
Tait, John 83, 85, *86*
Tait, John Murray 85
Tait, Peter 28
Tait, William 94, 124
Tait's Lodberry 66
Taylor, Provost J. J. 62
Thomason, Laurence T. 79
Thomson, Peter 117
Thomson, Sinclair 101
Thule Bar 66
Thule Hotel 124
Tolbooth xvi, 62, 75, *77*, 81, *81*, *82*, *83*, 84, *84*, 89, 91, *91*, 93–8, *95*, 99, *106*
Toll Clock Shopping Centre 96, *97*, 98
Torrie's house xvi, 16, 42, 45, *46*, 51, *52*, 53, *54*, 65, 89
Town Hall 63, 96, *103*, 116
Town's Park No. 8 101
Tulloch, Alexander I. 79, 80
Tulloch, Christie 57
Tulloch, Jasmine 58, *58*
Tulloch, Laurence *87*
Tulloch of Shetland 79, 80, 123
Turk's Head Public Bar 142
Turnbull family 46

Turnbull, Rev. John 42, 46, 66, 71
Turnbull-Stewart, Miss Grace M. S. 42, 46, 67, 71, 117, 118
Twageos 15–18, *15*, *21*, 23, *23*, 25, 53, 87, 94, 119
Twageos Camp 19–20, *20*
Twageos House 15–18, *15*, *16*, *17*, *18*, 19, 21, 53, 87
Twageos Road 17, 19, 21, *22*, 24
Twageos Social Club 20, *20*, 21, 23
Tyrie, William 128

Union Street 102
United Free Church 115, 116
United Presbyterian Church 100, 115

Valk, Rev. L. van der 5, 6, 10, *10*, 115
Vance, James 128
Vegte, G. H. van de 6, 117–18
Verstraeten, Theophilus 122
Vetvik, Astrid and Reidar 35, 36, *36*
Victoria Building *105*
Victoria Pier 40, *66*, 77, 106, 135
Victoria Restaurant 138, *138*

Waldie, Rev, Thomas, and family 45–6
Walker, Rev. Robert 101
Walker's School 101
Wallace, Rev. Derek 32
Water Lane xvi, 67, 69–72, *69*, *72*
Wesley manse *101*
West Hall 11
Westside Pine shop 65
White, Miss 32
Whitegates *54*
Widows' Homes *15*, 39, *39*, 56
Wilkins, Mr and Mrs Neil 123
Williamson, Attie 79
Williamson, Daniel Rendall 90
Williamson, Frank 133
Williamson, Grizel 51
Williamson, Irene and Jim 58, *58*, 59, *59*
Williamson, John (Johnnie Notions) 12, *12*
Williamson, Laurence 45
Williamson, Linda *58*
Williamson, Mrs Mimie 79
Winchester family members *21*
Wingate, John 26
Wishart, Basil 47

Wright, Billy and Sheila *21*
Wünsche, W. L. 100

Yates, Mrs Elizabeth J., shop *135*, 136–7, *136*
Yates's lodberry 73, 76, 78, *78*
Younger, Malcolm 118

Zetland Hotel 122, 124